AF568136

WOMEN WORKERS IN UNORGANIZED SECTOR

WOMEN WORKERS IN UNORGANIZED SECTOR

By

Dr. A. Selvakumar

M.Com., M.Phil., M.B.A., Ph.D.
Principal
Pope's College (Autonomous)
Sawyerpuram - 628 251
Thoothukudi District - Tamilnadu
(India)

DISCOVERY PUBLISHING HOUSE PVT. LTD.
INDIA

Published by:
Namit Wasan

DISCOVERY PUBLISHING HOUSE PVT. LTD.
4383/4B, Ansari Road, Darya Ganj
New Delhi-110 002 (India)
Phone : +91-11-23279245; 23253475; 43596065
E-mail : discoverybooksindia@gmail.com
discoverypublishinghouse@gmail.com
namitwasan9@gmail.com
web : www.discoverypublishinggroup.com

First Edition: **2019**

ISBN: 978-93-88854-11-5

Women Workers in Unorganized Sector

Printed at:
Infinity Imaging Systems
Delhi

Foreword

The changing economic scenario and social demands have remoulded the nature of work throughout the world. In India, for a long time, the business activities are exclusively the prerogative of male family members and for women child bearing and child rearing are the sole occupations. Conditions changed after the independence, in the course of implementation of five year plans, onslaught of globalization, development of women education, and the advent of technology-all have paved a way for women entrepreneurship and their entry to all kinds of business/industry activities. Amid this backdrop, the book authored by Dr. A Selvakumar, i.e, "Women Wokers in Unorganised Sector" has assumed greater significance than ever before.

This book has branched off into eight chapters which are highly relevant to its title Dr. A. Selvakumar who got Ph.D. degree under my supervision on "Child Labour in Beedi making industry in Tirunelveli District" has already authored a book on "Child Labour in home based sector" in 2005. He has undertaken a number of projects on child and women labour. With his vast administrative and research experience, now he has brought out "Women Workers in Unorganised Sector" which is actually based on his research project.

This book would be very useful to those working in the field of women entrepreneurship and training as well as for embaring on research on women work force and entrepreneurship. I congratulate Dr. A. Selvakumar for bringing out in this edition the latest developments in the field.

Dr. R. NEELAMEGAM
Emeritus Professor
Research Centre in Business Administration
VHNSN College (Autonomous)
Virudhunagar - 626 001
Tamilnadu

Preface

At the outset, I praise Almighty God Jesus Christ for having showered His blessing on me to bring out this book. Without Him, this humble piece of work would not have been successfully published as book.

In India, readymade garment industry is one of the largest export industries. Garment workers, in our country and obviously around the world, who do the basic stichings of children-wears and women's garments are predominantly women. Moreover, in our area, garment production at home is often an option for the poor and least educated rural women. Being one of the oldest industries with a history of more than 150 years, India stand second interms of export of total quantity of readymade garments and garment materials.

In recent times, many academic institutions and universities have integrated rural women employment and garment industries in their core curriculum of UG and PG and research courses. On this basis the author has written this book for the use of commerce students of UG and PG courses and scholars of commerce research and also as a hand book for the rural garment industrialists. The chief aim of the author is to give a systematic account of the unorganized rural industry and the poor village women as its workforce.

After publishing my book on "Child Labour in Home Based Sector" and the two edited volumes entitled, "Plight of Unorganised Workers" and "Status of Unorganised Labour, I received many appreciations and suggestions. Most of them were very encouraging and inspiring. This led me to publish this book entitled, "Women Workers in Unorganised Sector".

Suggestion for upgrading the content and style shall be highly appreciated from teachers students and researchers.

I express my gratitude to Dr. R. Neelamegam, Emeritus Professor, former Professor and Head, Department of Corporate Secretaryship, Alagappa University, Karaikudi and Director, Research Centre in Business Administration, V.H.N.S.N. College (Autonomous), Virudhunagar, Tamilnadu for having consented to write foreword of this book. His useful comments and suggestions encouraged me immensely to bring out this book.

My sincere thanks to Dr. G. Karunanithi, former Professor and Head, Department of Sociology, Manonmaniam Sundaranar University, Tirunelveli, Tamilnadu for his kind motivation and guidance to publish this book.

I sincerely thank, the former Bishop The Rt. Rev. Dr. Jason S. Dharmaraj and former Principal and Secretary of Pope's College, Prof. K. Paul Dawson for appointing me as Asst. Prof. of Commerce in our college and their kind encouragement in my early days of my career.

I would like to convey my sincere gratitude to our former Bishop The Rt. Rev. Dr. J.A.D. Jebachandran and our former Secretary Advocate J.Jeyasingh Thiyagaraj Natterji, M.P. (LS) to elevate me as Principal of this elite institution and their kind encouragement and support in my career development.

Also, my sincere thanks to our former Bishop The Rt. Rev. Dr. S. Jeyapaul David, Rev. M. Rajasekaran, Rev. J.S. Anand Asir and Rev. V.M.S. Tamilselvan for their prayerful support to elevate me as the Principal of Pope's College.

I heartily thank our Bishop The Rt. Rev. Dr. S.E.C. Devasagayam, Chairman and Secretary of Pope's College, for his kind encouragement and prayerful support to publish this book.

I am thankful to Mr. S.D.K. Rajan, Lay Secretary, Thoothukudi Nazareth Diocese and Auditor J. Jebachandran, Secretary Standing Committee on Collegiate Education, TND and former CSI Moderator's Commissary & former Secretary of Pope's College Rev. D. JesuSahayam for their kind encouragement to publish this book.

I express my profound sense of gratitude to Prof. G. Mohamed Pasi, Former Principal, Sadakathullah Appa College, Tirunelveli, Dr. J. Balasingh, former Principal and Secretary, St.John's College, Tirunelveli and Major T.J.T. Rajkumar, former Principal and Secretary, Pope's College, Sawyerpuram for their encouragement to concentrate on my research work in my early days. It led to me bring out this book.

I am grateful to University Grants Commissions for granting financial assistance to undertake three Minor Research Projects and two Major Research Projects. Also, I thank UGC for encouraging me to publish this book.

I must express my sincere thanks to Dr. P. Duraipalam Thanasingh, former Head, Department of Zoology, Pope's College, Sawyerpuram and Dr. R. Immanuel, Vice-Principal, Pope's College, for their valuable help and solid support to bring out this book.

I would like to convey my thanks to Dr. H. Johnson Jeyakumar, Controller of Examinations, Pope's College, Mr. J. Johnson Asir, Bursar, Dr. R. Selvakumar, Dean of Arts, Dr. C. Ravi Samuel Raj, Dean of Research, Dr. J. Christopher Raja, Asst. Prof. of English, and Dr. T. ChibiChelliah, Principal, Bishop Caldwell College, Dr. J. Jeyasingh, Former HOD of Economics, Dr. D. Jeyasingh, Principal, Mano Constituent College, Nagalapuram, Mr. A. Thangamani and Mr. V. Asirvatham for their encouragement to publish this book.

I also thank my colleagues Dr. J. Arulraj Daniel, Dean of Students Service, Dr. Mrs. D. Annie Angel Mercy, Mrs. J. Sheeba Princes, Mrs. S. Dayana Sweetlin, Mrs. E. Sheeba, Mr. J. Ponsam, Mrs. M. Subha, Mrs. S. Usha Rani, Mrs. S. Sangeetha, Mr. P. Finny Christadoss, Mr. G. JabezRajan, Mrs. T. Annakili& Mrs. T. AnithaRajathi for their prayerful support.

I thank Dr. V. Duraisingh, Asst. Prof. of Economics, Rani Anna Govt. Arts College, Tirunelveli, for his kind help in publishing this book.

I avail myself of this opportunity to express my deep sense of gratitude to my beloved parents, Mr. D. Ayyapillai and Late Mrs. A. Mariammal, my elder brother Dr. A. Arul Devadoss, in-laws Mr. N. Francis, Mrs. Leela Francis, Late Mr. F. Godwin and Mr. F. Suresh Jesuwin.

My dear wife Mrs. Graceline Julia Selvakumar, Beloved daughter Mrs. S. Letishia Mary Jebasingh & loving Son-in-law Auditor S. Jebasingh and beloved younger daughter S. Ida Blessy were silent and prayerful upholders to me to publish this book.

I am thankful to Mr. Tilak Wasan, Director, Discovery Publishing House Pvt. Ltd., New Delhi for his kind help and co-operation on publishing this book.

A. Selvakumar

Contents

1

Introduction

The birth of readymade garment industry dates back to 1818 when the first cotton mill was established at Fort Gloster near Calcutta with English Capital. The real growth of the industry however, started with the setting up of the Bombay Spinning and Weaving Mills in 1856. The progress of the industry in its initial stages was far from smooth.

The organized cotton textile industry is one of our oldest and most firmly established major industries. The industry had assets worth Rs. 1,300 crores. In 1982, there were 805 mills in the industry with nearly 22.5 million spindles and over 2.1 lakh looms. The total output of the mills was valued at Rs.3,600 crores. The industry provided direct employment to 11.5 lakh workers accounting for 18 percent of all factory labour totaling 60 lakh workers. Being one of the oldest industries it has a history of over 150 years. It occupies a unique position in the world export market where India is second only to Japan in terms of total quantity of export and supplies 16 per cent of the world exports.

Inspite of the opening of several textile in other parts of the country, more than 60 per cent of the existing spindles and looms are concentrated in Maharashtra and Gujarat, Bombay, Ahmedabad, Sholapur, Kanpur, Nagpur, Indore, Madurai, Coimbatore which are the main centres of this industry.

The Swadeshi Movement and the First World War materially changed the structure of the mills, and many mills were set up with their own weaving departments in order to meet the growing demands of the local market. In 1930 the situation improved further as a result of bilateral trade agreements with Japan. When protection was granted in 1927, the industry began to make rapid progress.

WORKING WOMEN

A working woman in ready made garment industry has a more interesting life than the one who does not work and there is also the charm of a pay-pocket. To awaken the people, it is the women who must be awakened. Once she is on the move, the family moves, the village moves and the nation moves.

Women who constitute half of the world's population are not fully harnessed as a human resource. Women's participation is vital, in Indian scenario. Any society cannot go ahead if 50 percent of the population do not participate in its developmental activities. Indira Gandhi, the former Prime Minister of India observed that neglect of women would be criminal, since field humanity had been deprived of half of the energy and creative talents. Right through Indian history, in all religions and cultures, women have been assigned a secondary status (Shakuntala Balaraman, 1986).

The world wars proved to be a turning point in the history of mankind. The participation of women in the work force started increasing since then. This trend is observed in developing nations (Kalpana Sharma, 1988).

In tune with the world wide trend, Indian women are marching towards self development. In India, women played a secondary role for centuries. During the colonial role, women lived a miserable and horrible life in diverse situations (Krishna Murthy, 1999).

The socio-economic changes that were set in motion in India after independence provided women with better educational and employment opportunities. Besides, a series of laws such as the Special Marriage Act 1954, The Hindu

Marriage Act 1955, Equal Remuneration Act 1976 passed by the Government of India helped to improve a lot of women. Today educated Indian women have made a landmark in the non-conventional fields like consultancy, marketing, advertising, garment works and exporting, beauty parlors, road and building construction. Women have started coming forward in considerable number in certain spheres of higher category jobs like civil service, judiciary, foreign Service, medicine and architecture. In organized sectors like banking, insurance, communication and air transport women's share in employment has recently doubled over the decade and government's intervention played an important role in this regard (Nirmala Banerjee , 1989).

Women are the heart of development. They control most of the non-money economy (subsistence agriculture, bearing and caring children, domestic labour) and take an important part in the money economy (trading, the "informal latter' wage employment). Everywhere in the world women have two jobs-around the home and outside it.

Women are half the world's population and they receive one-tenth of the world's income, account for two-thirds of the world's working hours, and own only one hundred of the world's prosperity. The process of Industrialization, urbanization and the increased educational and employment opportunities for women have brought about changes in the traditional attitudes and values of urban women in India.

The role of women in our society even as career women, not to speak of house holders is not insignificant. They have played a significant role in the socio-economic and political development of our country. The old order which confined women to the home as servants and helpers to their men folk, is being replaced now by a new one in which women increasingly undertake to fulfill many roles, within the homes as wives, mothers and home makers and outside it, as partners and co-workers of men in all types of enterprises. The few fortunate women who have the benefits of higher education seem to be quite obvious of their immense responsibilities for the emancipation of the women in the country side and of the working and middle class families in urban areas. The production side of women's work at home is gradually decreasing leading to a reduction of woman's role at home. Women perceive more and more clearly that if they really want to contribute to the welfare of their family and society the most effective way is to go out of home and earn money (Sumit Gupta et al., 1989).

Presently, educational, political, economic and social changes have changed women's status, their roles and way of life greatly. But this could also change their feminine character a little. Indeed they work, but they work for the family that too, from economic impulses. They extend support to their family. The working women, on the whole, never sought to sublimate or bypass the demands of family life. Rather their homes and families have either come first, or have stood at par with their work. This role is very significant, as far as the art of maintaining a stable family life, and thereby a stable society is concerned.

Traditionally women's occupational status has always been closely associated with the home and family. She has only a secondary status because she is economically dependent on her father or husband (Mary Billington, 1991).

In order in improve the status and position of women at home and in the society at large, it is necessary to achieve economic independence for women. Women are employed in all fields. They are shouldering official, family and social burdens.

Working women can be defined as the employed women ranging from those who are employed in small scale industries and organizations to those who, possess ownership and authority in organizations in government, private and quasi-government sectors (Lawrence Mary , 1998).

Working women could be brought under three categories in socio-economic basis. The first category includes agricultural workers and those who engage in traditional menial services, construction work and domestic works such as cleaning, cooking and washing.

The Second category mostly consists of those women who work in offices or in factories. They can be called the blue-collar women workers.

The third category of women workers are well educated. They are quite well off in life. They have both vertical and horizontal mobility.

In general, women's participation in industrial activities particularly in readymade garment industry shows their concern on family development and thereby the development of the country.

STATEMENT OF THE PROBLEM

The status of women is closely associated with their economic position, which in turn, depends upon their access to productive resources of the country and the opportunities for participation in economic activities.

Female population in Thoothukudi District is greater in number than the males, but they are more backward in the matter of literacy and employment level. Women workers in Thoothukudi District are facing a number of problems on the work spot, which vociferously demand an investigative study.

People particularly women form the real wealth of a nation. The process of development, in a broad sense, should ensure social and economic opportunities and equal share of human rights to all people. Women cannot be denied the opportunities of rights and participating in the benefit offered by the government. The magnitude of women workers as revealed by the census publications show that not less than 10 million women are engaged in some form of economic activity or the other at any given time. Poverty compels the low income and poor households to opt for women's work so that their wages are important to support the family.

Women in India have always been participating in economic activities in one form or the other. In the olden days, when families followed the same occupation generation after generation, women helped their husbands/family to generate the major income and run the family.

In the contemporary context, extreme poverty has created a situation in which women also have to be part of hired labour and earn wages for themselves and for their family. Workforce is thus separated from the family environment depriving the women the protection and guidance of their husbands. In this study an attempt has been made to study the socio-economic condition, the employment condition, exploitation, demand and supply and occupation hazards/diseases of the women workers in readymade garment works in Thoothukudi district and Tamil Nadu.

SIGNIFICANCE OF THE STUDY

This study is purely women centred. Women in position, can act as catalysts in develop processes. It is felt that the social status of women is considered to be one of the factors that are related to fertility and of the population growth[1]. Women's participation brings about development.

Nashah has conducted a study on women workers in an un-organized sector in Kashmir. The overall analysis of data also unveils the fact that inadequate income, illiteracy and ignorance of parents in addition to the large family size are the precipitating factors, which drag young women into the world of labour. She also indicates that physical deformities and weak eyesight are the effects of early employment[2].

Jeyaraj in his research paper entitled "Labour Force Participation of Women and Children in Rural Tamil Nadu" explores the relevance of distress as the determinant of labour force participation of women and children. It has three dimensions, viz., level of income, distribution of income and stability of income or earnings. Identification or classification of the three dimensions of distress offers a convenient framework for analyzing the impact of various factors that determine the participation of women and children in the labour force. Apart from factors related to distress, to capture the impact of sociological factors, the percentage of Schedule Caste population in the total population has been introduced into the analysis. The analysis of the paper indicates that distribution of income and stability in earnings is the major determinant of the labour force participation of women and children. These results indicate the fallacy in relying solely on raising the level of income or the general level of prosperity to eradicate distress. Thus, the paper argues in favour of redistribution of resources, particularly land, which is considered as the most suitable policy measure in eradicating poverty and distress induced by forced participation of women and particularly children in the labour force[3].

Lalitha Devi in her paper "Status and Employment of women in India" examined the role of white collar employment in contributing to higher status among women. The author explains that the employment has given women an opportunity to shoulder responsibility, play new roles, react with new people, face new situations, etc., The effective performance of these new roles exploded the myth of female inferiority. They participate in socially meaningful and prestigious programmes[4].

From very early days woman took part in various agricultural operations, tea and coffee plantations, beedi and tobacco industry, jute and textile production, bonded labourers in brick kiln, stone quarries and at construction sites. Few took up self employment such as selling fish and recycling garbage. Some worked in the handlooms and power looms and as embroidery and zari workers"[5].

The studies discussed above are related in one way or the other to the present study. However, it differs from these studies in several respects. It has certain special features, which have been discussed in the succeeding section.

The present study would give primary importance to the contribution of the women workers to their family Income every month and to the levels of exploitation of women workers by employers.

The study also attempts to find out the extent to which the income of the family is increased due to the employment of women. Further, an attempt is made to study whether the husbands/family members from economically backward families force their women to work. Besides analyzing the working and living conditions of the women workers, a special focus has been to be given on the impact of legal intervention and occupation hazards in women employment.

The discipline of commerce includes labour studies as one of the important areas of interest, Female Labours/women workers form a part of labour studies. In recent times, it has drawn the attention of academicians, planners and administrators all over the world.

OPERATIONAL DEFINITION

The researcher presents the specific operational definition of this phenomenon under study as follows:

Women garment worker may be defined as a woman at above 15 age performing any activity relating to readymade garments on regular basis with or without remuneration. They may carry out the work in the shop/industry/unit.

This comprehensive study focuses on the women of the age of 15 years and above, who are employed in readymade garment works of various kinds in and around the village Puthiyamputhur, situated in Thoothukudi District of Tamil Nadu.

OBJECTIVES OF THE STUDY

In view of the observations made during the pilot survey, the following objectives have been formulated:

1. to understand the demand and supply factors involved in the employment of women;
2. to know the working conditions of women workers;
3. to find out the extent of exploitation of women workers; and
4. to study the occupational hazards of women workers.

In order to fulfill these objectives, the women workers from readymade garment works are to be selected from various readymade garment shops engaged in different types of work.

HYPOTHESES OF THE STUDY

The following five hypotheses are formulated:

1. There is no significant difference between age limit and income generation in readymade garment work.
2. There is no significant difference between age limit and health problems of the women workers in readymade garment works.
3. There is no significant difference between educational status and job satisfaction of women workers of readymade garment works.
4. There is no significant difference between quantum of income of women workers and job satisfaction.
5. There is no significant difference between marital status and job satisfaction of women workers of readymade garment works.

METHODOLOGY

Area of the Study

Thoothukudi district of Tamil Nadu has been taken as the area of study. This comprises of three revenue divisions namely Thoothukudi, Kovilpatti and Tiruchendur. Thoothukudi district was purposively selected as the study area for two reasons. First, the district has a large number of readymade garment units and women workers. The second reason is that, the researcher is familiar with the area and so is able to get the cooperation of the officials and also the respondents.

Thoothukudi is a city and it remains as a corporate body in Tamil Nadu. Marine fishery, pearl and chunk fishing are famous in this district from time immemorial. The city is also known as "Pearl city". It is a seaport which serves southern Tamil Nadu including the inland cities of Tirunelveli, Nagercoil, Virudhunagar, Ramanathapuram, Madurai etc. It is one of the major sea ports in India with its history dating back to the 16th century.

ORIGIN OF THE NAME

There are three theories as to the origin of the name: Thoorthu (Dig) and Kudi (Drink)- The town has no rivers and the only source of drinking water was from wells. "Thoortha" means land "reclaimed" from sea while "Kudi" also stands for "settlement". Hence "Thoortha Kudi", later it became Thoothukudi. It could mean a settlement built on land reclaimed from sea. Now-a-days the city is called "Tuticorin" in English and "Thoothukudi" in Tamil.

Thoothukudi is traditionally known for its pearl fishery and shipbuilding. It became the centre of the Indian independence movement in the early 20th century, with leaders like Maaveeran Sundaralinga Kudumbanar, the famous Poet Subramanya Bharathi, Veerapandia Kattabomman, Vellaya Thevan and V.O.Chidambaram Pillai. In 1906, the freedom fighter Shri.V.O.Chidambaram Pillai, with the help of Shri Bala Gangadhar Tilak, launched the first Swadeshi ship *"S.S. Gaelia"* from this port town in British India. The revolutionary Vanchinathan was also the proud soul of the soil.

GEOGRAPHY

Thoothukudi is located in South India about 540 km to the south west of Chennai. This district is bounded on the north by the districts of Virudhunagar and Ramanathapuram on the east and south-east by Gulf of Mannar and on the west and south-west by the districts of Tirunelveli and Kanyakumari. The total area of this district is 4,621sq.km. According to the 2011census, the Thoothukudi district had a population of 17,38,376 persons of which 8,58,919 were males and 8,79,457 were females. (Census Report, 2011) The administrative headquarters is an urban agglomeration and also one of the taluk headquarters within the district. The district of Thoothukudi was carved out as a separate district in the year 1986 as a result of bifurcation of the Tirunelveli district of Tamil Nadu State.

Apart from the three revenue divisions, eight taluks and twelve blocks are there in the district. This district also comprises of 19 town panchayats, two municipalities and one corporation. There are 480 revenue villages grouped in 408 village panchayats. Seven assembly and one parliamentary constituencies are available in the district (Records of the District Revenue Office, 2011).

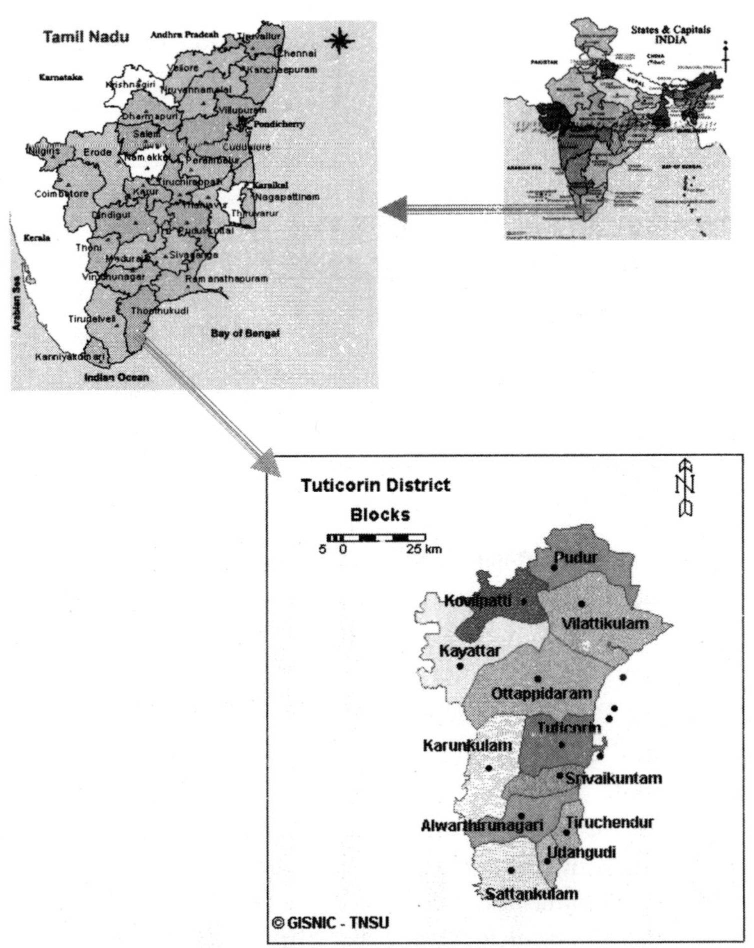

Map: 1.1 – Area of Study

CLIMATE AND RAINFALL

The climate of Thoothukudi is neither too hot nor too cold. During the months of April, May and June the Thoothukudi district remains hot. During winter, in the months of December and January, the climate is pleasant.

Table 1.1

Seasonwise Rainfall during 2009-2010 in Thoothukudi District

Season	Period	Normal Rainfall (mm)	Actual (mm)
Winter Period	Jan-Feb	46.6	47.9
Hot weather Period	March to May	112.2	66.4
South West monsoon	June to September	86.8	54.5
North East Monsoon	Oct to December	410.1	490.5
Total		655.7	659.3

Source: District Statistical Hand Book 2009-2010, Thoothukudi District.

The maximum temperature is 35.7° C and the minimum is 24.4° C. The rainfall is high in the coastal taluks of Thoothukudi and Tiruchendur. The normal rainfall of the district is 655.7 mm but the actual rainfall varies from year to year, and the variation is small (District Statistical Hand Book 2009-2010).

Table 1.1 reveals the rainfall in Thoothukudi district during 2009-10. When the North East Monsoon started, the actual rainfall was higher that is, 490.5 millimetres. During the winter period the actual rainfall was very low that is, 47.9 millimetres.

LANGUAGE

There is a traditional belief that the Tamil language originated from the *Pothigai Malai*, a hill situated in Western Ghats near Papanasam, a small village in the Tirunelveli district. As per Brahminical legend, Lord Shiva sent the two saints Vyasa and Agatyar (in *Sanskrit Aastya*) to create the divine languages Sanskrit and Tamil. Agatyar came to Papanasam and established the Tamil culture from the Pothigai Malai.

Today the Tamil language as spoken in the Tirunelveli district is called Nellai Tamil. Since Tamil was born in Pothigai Malai, the Nellai Tamil is the first form of Tamil and also the pure form. It is the very sweetest form of Tamil. Nellai Tamil is very fast while compared to other forms of spoken Tamil. The version spoken here is considerably different from others.

LITERACY

The literacy rate in Thoothukudi district is explained in the following table.

Table 1.2

The Literacy Rate as per 2009-2010 Report of Thoothukudi District

Category	Literacy Rate (%)		
	Male	Female	Total
Tamil Nadu	82.33	64.55	73.47
Thoothukudi	77.00	67.00	72.00

Source: Tamil Nadu – An Economic Appraisal, 2009-2010, Department of Evaluation and Applied Research (DEAR) Government of Tamil Nadu, Chennai, pp.S4 – S5.

EMPLOYMENT

The total workers in the district are 6,78,811, out of which male workers are 4,31,784 and female workers are 2,47,027 in numbers. The rural workers are 4,32,127 while urban workers are 2,46,684. The employment pattern shows that there are 67,307 cultivators, 1,23,988 landless agricultural labourers, 35,483 persons in household industry and 3,61,818 persons are categorized as other workers. There are 90,215 marginal workers and 89,346 non-workers (District Statistical Hand Book 2009-2010).

IRRIGATION

There are no big reservoirs in this district. So, the different sources of irrigation are channels, tanks and wells which cover 45,673 hectares; of which 19,493 hectares are covered by wells. The Papanasam and Manimuthar dams located in the Tirunelveli district under Tamirabarani River Irrigation systems are the main sources of irrigation. Other than the Tamirabarani River, the river *Vaipar* in Vilathikulam taluk, the river *Karumeni* which traverses through Sathankulam and Tiruchendur taluks are the sources of water. In Ottapidaram taluk there is one small reservoir at Eppodumvendran village.

INDUSTRY IN THOOTHUKUDI

Thoothukudi has a host of industries including power, chemicals, fisheries and IT. They are Can Do Automation (Industrial Automation Experts), Sterlite Copper Smelter, SPIC - Fertilizer Plant, Thoothukudi Thermal Power Plant, Thoothukudi Alkali Chemicals, Heavy Water Plant, Dharangadhara Chemical Works (DCW), Kilburn Chemicals, Madura Coats, Thoothukudi Spinning Mills, Ramesh Flowers, Nila Sea Foods, Diamond Sea Foods, Salt Industries, CTPL (Coco Tufters Pvt. Ltd.), Venus Home Appliances, Hitech Flyash India (P) Ltd, Threekay Solutions Pvt. Ltd., (Call Center) and Jesus Soft (Software Development Company).

Tata Steel has been trying to set up titanium dioxide project in Thoothukudi. The project outlay is about Rs.2,500 crores. Besides, there are availability of skilled labour, electricity generating plants and a container facility. A major port has also come to existence. Thoothukudi is one of the major centres for industry and business in Tamil Nadu. The Sethusamudram project, the airport at Vagaikulam, Koodankulam Nuclear Power plant, improvised road and railway infrastructure and Nanguneri SEZ are expected to make Thoothukudi an attractive choice for business investment.

AGRICULTURE

Out of the total area of 4,70,724 hectares in the district 1,78,083 hectares are brought under crop cultivation. The main crop in the district is paddy. Paddy is cultivated in the Srivaikundam, Sattankulam and Tiruchendur taluks. *Cumbu, Cholam, Kuthiraivali* and other pulses are raised in the dry tracts of Kovilpatti, Vilathikulam, Ottapidaram and Thoothukudi taluks. Cotton is largely cultivated in Kovilpatti, Ottapidaram and Thoothukudi taluks. Groundnut cultivation is undertaken in Kovilpatti, Tiruchendur and Sattankulam taluks.

Palmyrah trees are grown mostly in Tiruchendur, Srivaikundam, Sattankulam and Vilathikulam taluks. Jaggery is produced from palmyrah juice which is the main occupation of the village people of Tiruchendur and Sattankulam taluks. Banana and other vegetables are raised in Srivaikundam and Tiruchendur taluks.

SALT PRODUCTION

The district alone constitutes 70 per cent of the total salt production of Tamil Nadu. The share of total salt production of India is 30 per cent.

TRANSPORT AND COMMUNICATION

The important towns and villages are well connected with a good network of roads. The total length of roads in the Thoothukudi district is 4,705 kms., out of which the length of the surfaced and the unsurfaced is 4,556.373 and 148.698 km respectively. The length of the National Highways in the Thoothukudi district is 118.80 km and that of the State Highways is 1,988.664 km. Municipality and Municipal Corporation roads contribute a length of 283.12 km. Panchayat and panchayat union covers the length of 2,274.52 km. and town panchayat and township road constitute a length of 506.08 km. The district has a 96 km length of railways. Thoothukudi is connected by Air transport from June 1991 and the airport is located near Vagaikulam at a distance of 15 kms from Thoothukudi city.

THERMAL POWER PLANT

The Thoothukudi Thermal Power Plant is the biggest power station in Tamil Nadu with five 210 Megawatt generators. The first generator was commissioned in July, 1979. This power station supplies about one-third of the total power demand of Tamil Nadu.

SHIPPING

Thoothukudi has been a centre for maritime trade and pearl fishery for more than a century. Its natural harbour with a rich hinterland, facilitated development of the port. Thoothukudi was declared as a minor anchorage port in 1868. In 1906, V.O. Chidambaram Pillai launched the first swadeshi ship *S.S. Gaelia* in British India from Thoothukudi Port. After Independence, the minor Port of Thoothukudi witnessed a flourishing trade and handled a variety of cargo.

To cope with the increasing trade through Thoothukudi, the Government of India sanctioned the construction of an all-weather Port at Thoothukudi. On 11 July 1974, the newly-constructed Thoothukudi port was declared to be the tenth major port in India. Thoothukudi Port is an artificial one. This is the third international port in Tamil Nadu. The port is also helping increase the tourism in the region. A new ferry has been commenced between Thoothukudi and Colombo.

Thoothukudi is one of the very few ports of India where mechanised sailing vessels are operated. These vessels are operated at the Old Port which is termed by the port authorities as Zone B.

FISHERIES

Marine fishing, Pearl and Valamburi *Chunk* fishing are famous in this district from the time immemorial. Thoothukudi is the main centre for deep sea fishing in the district which has a lengthy coast-line of about 140 km. Prawn culture was important and earned a considerable amount of foreign exchange. Now the prawn culture has been banned by the Supreme Court of India due to pollution issues. Thoothukudi Fishing industry thrives well, since this is the place known to attract varieties of fish daily unlike other centres. Fishes caught here are either sold locally or exported. *Tuna* which is caught here is dried and sold as *Maasi*. Dry fish from Thoothukudi is sent to Sri Lanka and many parts of South India. The fish-cake produced here are used as food for prawns and other fishes. There are 11 marine fishing villages.

There is one Joint Director of Fisheries and Assistant Directors of Fisheries in charge of *Pearl-chunk* fishing, Fishermen Training Institute and for technical guidance. There is fish-seed farm at Kadamba. Service centre/Base workshop of this district is situated at Thoothukudi. Fish is produced and supplied to the poor at cheaper rates. There is a fish curing centre at Palayakayal. There are 450 mechnaised boats, 1300 vallams and 900 *Kattamarans* in this district. About 5,428 Fishermen families are directly engaged in fishing in these vessels. There is a Fisheries College and Research Centre at Thoothukudi. The estimated inland fish catch is 1,583 MT and Marine fish catch is 34,066 MT in the year 1999.

OTTAPIDARAM

Ottapidaram is the biggest taluk in Tamil Nadu state, India. It is a small town in Thoothukudi District. Ottapidaram continues to be a tourism centre, but has accessibility with many places from Tamil Nadu. One can reach Tirunelveli or Tuticorin easily from anywhere and Ottapidaram is very close to these two places (45 km from Tirunelveli and 22 km from Thoothukudi). It is the birth Place of the Freedom Fighter Maveeran Sundaralinga Kudumbanar and V.O.Chidambaram pillai, fondly called as VOC. He is also called as *"Kappalottiya Tamizhan"* because he only launched the first shipping company which operated ships between Thoothukudi and Colombo against the British during the British regime in India.

'Kollankinar' amongst the panchayats in Ottapidaram taluk is famous in the taluk for its agricultural activities. The surrounded areas are *Vanchi Maniyachi* south east about 1.2 km, the railway junction connecting Tirunelveli and Tuticorin. The railways will connect in 45 minutes of journey to each of the corporation cities. (Tirunelveli and Thoothukudi) Southern Railways has laid down double line for smooth to and fro movement of trains from Vilupuram to Thoothukudi and the other places from *"Vanchi Maniyachchi"* to Kanyakumari, since long years.

The main attractions in Ottapidaram are:

1. The house of V.O.C has been converted to a Library which houses some rare photographs of Sh.VOC
2. Ulagamman (Goddess) temple
3. Panchalankurichi is one other main attraction which is just 3 km from Ottapidaram. It houses a fort constructed by the Tamil Nadu government in the place of ruined fort constructed by *Veerapandiya Kattabomman,* the famous king who ruled this place in the 17th century and fought against the British colonial rule. Even the portions of ruined fort can be seen these.
4. Jakkammal temple in Panchalankurichi, dates back to the 17th century. This is the temple in which Veerapandiya Kattabomman has worshipped regularly.

THE MAIN AGRICULTURAL CROPS

The major crops of Thoothukudi district are bananas, rice, sugar cane, greengram (*pachchai payaru* or *paasi payaru* or *payirtham payaru* (Tamil), blackgram "*ulundhu*" in Tamil, cotton, sesame are the major cultivation... and there are more than nine types of plantations are practiced along with those major crops.

The people here are mostly farmers and allied business people, as well government employees are also living here. The people here are known for their genial bravery and courage in India.

HISTORY OF PUTHIAMPUTHUR

Puthiamputhur is a village of the Ottapidaram Taluk. It is situated on the road from Thoothukudi to Ottapidaram about 17 km from Thoothukudi and 4 kilo meters before Ottapidaram. It is said that weekly market used to be in this village and hence it got the name "Pothi Amanthoor", which in time began to be known as Puthiamputhur. People of different caste are doing agriculture in this village. Now ready made cloth production industries flourish in this area.

Traditionally Puthiamputhur was known for Weekly market for 'Goats'. Today it has grown as one of the Export Centres of Ready Made Garments in Southern Tamil Nadu. Garments are the new world of Puthiamputhur. There are many individually owned garment factories, to the extent for an demand of Textile Park. A new economy zone, good for the nearby village people, who are otherwise dependent on nature's favour for their fertile lands.

Puthiamputhur is one of important villages involved in manufacturing readymade cloths. The cloths are sent all over India.

It provides employment for more than 10,000 workers mostly hailing from near by villages for more than 10 years. Now-a-days 3000 labourers are doing readymade garment works; more than 1500 women workers are working in readymade garment fields.

PERIOD OF STUDY

The present study is mainly based on primary data. The field investigation work was carried out during the period of January 2011 to December 2011.

SAMPLING DESIGN

The universe of the present filed work consists of women ready made garments spread all over the Thoothukudi taluk of Thoothukudi district. There are approximately 11,248 women ready made garments spread all over this taluk. There has been considered as a unit for the study. Therefore, 1,000 women readymade garment workers engaged in garment making activities were selected by convenient sampling method.

A pre-tested questionnaire was used to collect data from the respondents. The collected data were edited in order to ensure that all the required information had been gathered and irrelevant information omitted. After editing, the data were classified and analysed. Appropriate statistical tools were used to analyse the data.

The poor women respondents do not have a proper record of their income and expenditure. They depend on their memory to supply information. Any lapse in their memory may have affected the results of the study. Also, they are hesitant to supply information about their assets, savings and debts.

TOOLS OF DATA COLLECTION

1. Interview - Schedule

The present study is an empirical one. Survey method was employed to collect data from women workers in readymade garment works and their employers. So, an interview-schedule was prepared and applied. The data used for the present study were mainly primary in nature. An interview schedule was prepared for the reason that the respondents, by and large were found to belong to low in literacy and they were found to be totally incapable of managing questionnaire. The questions in these sections were based on the objectives of the study. Field work for the present study was carried out personally by the researcher.

A pre-test schedule was administered to 100 respondents. It was later re-structured with some additions and deletions. The modified schedule thus prepared was used as a tool to collect data from the respondents.

Field work for the present study will be carried out personally by the researcher. The survey was conducted in several stages. The suggestions provided by the respondents were carefully recorded at the end of the schedule.

Analysis of Data

After the fieldwork, the data were carefully scrutinised and edited in order to ensure accuracy, consistency and completeness. Most of the analyses were based on the responses presented in the form of frequency tables. The data tabulated were systematically processed and interpreted on the basis of the objectives formulated. Most of the analyses were based on the relevant statistical tools such as percentages, averages, multiple regression and Gini Co-efficient.

Gini Co-efficient

To measure the inequality of the distribution of income of women ready made workers, Gini co-efficent (G) of the following formula was used:

$G = 1 - \Sigma Pi (Zi + Zi - 1)$

where

Pi = cumulative percentage of person

Zi = cumulative percentage of income

In order to determine the disparity in distribution of income among the women workers, the analysis of the distribution of households and income according to households income groups in the form of Lorenz curve was carried out. To strengthen the analysis, tables, bar diagrams, pie diagrams were used in the study.

2. Observation

The observation technique was applied to collect certain relevant information in order to facilitate the study. There were chances of certain delicate issues being left out in spite of the careful administration of interview-schedule. But, it was supplemented by observation. Through observation, the researcher was able to understand the working general conditions, the pressures on women workers imposed by their employers, the seriousness of the health problems of women workers in readymade garment works and the like.

3. Case - Study

In addition to these tools of data collection, case - study method was used to collect detailed information from experienced women workers and employer, who will be capable of giving certain interesting and relevant information. Moreover, a few less experienced women were also interviewed and treated as case-studies because they were more spontaneous. This qualitative information was found to enrich the study in several ways.

4. Collection of Secondary data

Various publications and reports was collected from the Ministry of Labour, New Delhi, V.V.Giri National Labour Institute, Noida, International Labour Office (ILO), New Delhi and Chennai, Ministry of Welfare, New Delhi, Ministry of Rural Development, New Delhi, Indian Council of Social Science Research, New Delhi, Institute of Labour Studies, Chennai, Ministry of Labour, Tamil Nadu, Madras Institute of Developmental Studies, Chennai, Tata Institute of Social Studies, Mumbai and other University Libraries.

In addition to the above, discussions were facilitated and views were shared with Non-Governmental organisations, Labour officers, Local Body Administrators, District Collector and Women Development Organizations.

DATA PROCESSING AND ANALYSIS

After the fieldwork, the filled-up schedules were thoroughly scrutinised and edited inorder to ensure accuracy, consistency and completeness. The researcher with the assistance of a computer was able to do the coding of data. The classification, tabulation and further statistical treatment of data were done with the aid of the computer. The data were both qualitative and quantitative in nature. The qualitative data were converted into percentages. Most of the analysis were based on the responses presented in the form of frequency tables. The data thus tabulated were systematically processed and interpreted on the basis of the objectives formulated. These interpretations were utilized to draw conclusions. The data were analyzed by using other appropriate statistical tests to examine the significance of association between the variables taken for the analysis.

IMPLICATIONS

It is hoped that this study besides highlighting working conditions, exploitation and health problems of women ready made garment workers. would also provide an overall view of the plight of child labour in such sectors. The findings of the study can be shared with NGO representatives and Welfare Department Officials working on eradication of child labour. Besides, the suggestions and recommendations of the proposed study would also help the administrators, activists, policy makers and NGOs in understanding the problems of children employed in readymade garment works and also enable them to act on it in such a way as to put an end to this problem. Moreover, this study would develop a training model, which would be an effective tool for creating awareness among the children employed in the readymade garment works about their legal rights in their place of work. The report of the study will also be submitted to the respective District Administrators and concerned department officials of the State and Central government

LIMITATIONS OF THE STUDY

Any study which depends on primary data will have its own limitations. The respondents may not have a proper record of their income and expenditure. They may depend on their memory to supply informations. Any lapse in their memory may have affected the results of the study. Also, they may hesitate to provide information about their assets, savings and indebtedness. However, adequate care was taken to obtain correct data in this study.

CHAPTER SCHEME

The report of the study has been divided into eight chapters.

The first chapter is the introduction and design of the study. It covers introduction to the study, importance of the study, scope, objectives of the study, methodology, period of study, limitation of the study and the chapter scheme of the thesis.

Chapter II presents the review of the related literature which is bifurcated into five parts. To study the women workers in readymade garments; and for comparing women workers in brick industry, match industry, construction work and in other non-farm works are also included.

The third chapter deals with the socio demographic characteristics of women workers in readymade garment works in the study. It deals with respondents' age, religion, education, marital status, occupation family size and housing pattern.

The fourth chapter is to analyze the income and expenditure, savings pattern of women workers in readymade garment works

The fifth chapter deals with the exploitation of women workers in readymade garment works in Thoothukudi district.

The sixth chapter covers job security and satisfaction aspects

The seventh chapter is the study of generalized analysis of the occupational hazards in readymade garment works.

The final chapter summarizes the conclusive findings of the study.

REFERENCES

1. K.P.Singh, "Status of Women and Populations Growth in India," Munishiram Manoharlal, New Delhi, 1999.
2. Nashah, "A Study of Women Workers in Unorganised Sector in Kashmir (Unpublished Ph.D., Thesis, Kashmir University, Srinagar, 1991), pp. 11-23.
3. GJavarai. "Labour Force Participation of Women and Children in Rural Tamil Nadu: An Analysis of the Inter-district Variability". (Working Paper No. 3, Madras Institute of Development Studies, Madras, 1993), p. 31.
4. Lalitha Devi, "Status and Employment of Women in India", B.R Publishing Corporation, Delhi, 1982.
5. Women's Research Centre, "A Study on Women Workers in the Four Textile Mills Around Calcutta", Women's Research Centre Publication, Calcutta, 1994, p. 3.

Review of Literature

GENERAL

To develop clarity and comprehension in any study, it is necessary first to review the various concepts, research methodologies and analytical tools used by researchers in earlier studies. Such an attempt would help the researcher to have better and precise understanding of the perspectives of the research problem and would also facilitate the researcher to modify and improve the present analytical framework in the right direction to suit the problem situation. The findings of earlier studies would help the researcher in setting the hypothesis and objectives and enable him to compare his own findings. This chapter briefly reviews the concepts, research methodologies, analytical tools and findings of the past studies, which are relevant to the present study.

The review is presented under the following headings for better perception and clarity. This chapter makes an endeavour to study the women workers in readymade garment industries, brick industry, match industry, construction works and other non-farm works of the study have been presented in this chapter.

REVIEW

Women Workers in Readymade Garment Industry

Knowledge is fast growing in the modern days in all fields. Many numbers of studies have been conducted by the government, universities and private institutions. The review of related studies enables the scholars to get an idea of his/her area of research further, it may also help him/her to identify the untouched aspects of the area under study. By going through the related studies, it is possible for the scholar to identify the areas, which require more attention. The researcher can carry on his/her study in a different manner from the already existing studies. Hence reviews of some selected studies are presented here with regard to the women readymade garment workers and women workers in other fields.

Debal K.Singharoy and Prava Agarwal (1969) on "Self Employment for Rural Women" have emphasized that self employment is required for the best utilization of the available but unexploited human resources. They also stressed that the spread of literacy and technical knowledge in rural areas will attract more and more women to self employment projects and such a situation is bound to bring sense of pride and dignity in the rural population.

Nicholas S. Hopkins (1978) in his study found that the tailoring of winter overcoats is a prosperous craft in the Tunisian town of Testour. This paper investigates the social organization of production and the economic situation of the craft. It pays special attention to changes in work place organization, credit, wages, and price fixation, and in marketing and its relationship to Tunis dealers. The paper provides some reflections on the articulation of domestic and capitalist modes of production and on the evolution of tailoring from a handicraft to a manufacture through a reformulation of the mode of cooperation.

Raka Gupta and Bibin Kumar Gupta (1987) on "Role of Women in Economic Development" have revealed that the rural women really contribute more time in income formation activities in comparison with men, but still their socio-economic conditions remain pitiful. If population control programmes are not vigorously pursued, any hope of improvement in the role of women in economic development cannot be ensured.

Nalinadevi and Jagathambal (2000) deal with health and financial problems faced by unorganised women workers. Their study was undertaken in Chinnathadagam area of Periyanayickem Palay block in Coimbatore district. Poor working conditions have been found to cause greater fatigue, negligence, absenteeism, indiscipline and subordination among the women workers. The conclusion is that their employers must take effective measures to improve the sanitary conditions to protect the women workers from infectious diseases. The central government can initiate income generating schemes to enable the women workers to have adequate income for maintaining their families.

Pradeep Agrawal (2001) in his article viewed that India's garment and textile exports are likely to face fresh challenges with the phasing out of the Multi-Fibre Arrangement by 2005, as well as several regional trade treaties, such as NAFTA. Strong concerted policy action is needed, following up on the abolition of small-scale industry reservation for the garment sector, to enable it to grow rapidly and to provide foreign exchange and employment in the Indian economy.

Ganesh (2002) in an article reveals that the Indian textile industry is too fragmented and obsolete to benefit from the market openings which will follow the elimination of quota restraints. Evasion of excise duty is the basis of competitive advantage in the domestic textile industry, and this has driven the better units in the organised sector away from the domestic market into exports. But exporting units are vulnerable if they are deprived of access to the domestic market. It may be too late for government to untangle the knots it has created, but at least the 2002-03 budget proposals are a step in the right direction.

Manipal (2004) in his study "Social Development of rural Women in India" discusses the social development status of woman particularly in term of their general health and nutrition, sex ratio, education and physical quality because these aspects of their development and capacity building are reproductive actions in Indian Society economy.

Deepita Chakravarty (2004) in the literature on the gender implications of expansion of markets for employment often looks at women workers as the victims of the trade liberalization process, resulting from discrimination in the labour market. However, discrimination is a complex process taking different forms in different contexts leading to different outcomes. This study, based on the garment manufacturing industry, suggests that in the context of a dynamic industrial activity of a poor labour-surplus economy, discrimination against women can take place outside the labour market. For example, employment depends on education and skills, to which women have unequal access.

Deepita Chakravarty (2004) in her paper concluded that the literature on the gender implications of expansion of markets for employment often looks at women workers as the victims of the trade liberalization process, resulting from discrimination in the labour market. However, discrimination is a complex process taking different forms in different contexts leading to different outcomes. This study, based on the garment manufacturing industry, suggests that in the context of a dynamic industrial activity of a poor labour-surplus economy, discrimination against women can take place outside the labour market. For example, employment depends on education and skills, to which women have unequal access.

Arul Kamaraj and Muralitharan (2005) have studied about unorganized women in match industries of Virudhunagar. Their study explains that the women are considered as the human resource of choice for the unorganized sector because of lack of education and training and are amenable to accept lower wages for equal work due to gender casting. It is no longer possible to maintain a decent standard of life unless both husband and wife earn in a family so the unorganized sector contributes a lot to women to supplement their family income. They conclude that the employers make their working condition conductive by extending help to women workers, personal problems and redressing their grievances frequently and education is crucial for determining the better development path for the unorganized workers.

Kamalakannan (2005) in his study deals with women construction workers in Tamilnadu. His study analysed socio-economic conditions, wage and working conditions of women workers in construction work in Tuticorin. He suggested that the workers are advised to follow the small size family plan. Workers are provided with one-day holiday with pay and NGOs and Trade union take measures to educate them and self help groups are to be formed among women workers and financial assistance shall be provided for undertaking building contract work. He concluded that women below poverty line have to perform domestic duties and also supplement the family income by going to work. Since they are unskilled and illiterate they are subject to economic exploitation with low and discriminated wages. Government officials take measure for the payment of minimum wages to women workers and for the safety and security of women workers.

"The role of self help groups in fisher women development" is a work by Jayaraman and others (2005). They conducted a study on self groups in Punnakkayal during the year 2000-2001. They say that economic progress could be achieved through economic and social development. Punnakayal has a large number of self help groups. There are about 50 self help group members who are fishermen. Information was collected by personal interview schedule. Till 20th May 1998, 36 self help groups were formed, of which five were liked with bank which advanced Rs.97,500 to them. Moreover they concluded that the fishermen self help groups are found to be performing well and with necessary support from the Lead bank, NABARD and the Government. They could liberate themselves from the clutches of money-lenders, save adequate money for meting emergency expenditure, for productive investment and asset creation. It would also contribute to high literacy and socio-economic development.

Supriya Roy Chowdhury (2005) in her paper reveals that wages and working conditions in Bangalore's rapidly expanding garments export sector, employing a large number of women, remain completely unregulated. Governments and mainstream trade unions have been largely indifferent to this sector. A number of NGOs and new trade unions have now stepped into this vacuum. Their framework of activism focuses on development of a certain kind - credit associations, slum or neighbourhood development, internationalizing the issue of workers' rights - rather than on confrontational struggles over wages and working conditions. This genre of activism is based on a broad understanding of the informal sector, where a large number are self-employed, as one in which the employer-employee or capital-labour relationship is opaque, if not absent. However, this understanding and activism may indeed be limited in a context where capital is internationalized and labour is recast, into contractual, casualised, and in this case, feminized, workforce.

Anuradha Kalhan (2008) in his paper remarked that a sample survey of the Bangalore-based suppliers of ready-made garments to Wal-Mart Stores and other corporate retailers, together with meetings with some of their workers suggests that, among other ways, these suppliers deal with the tendency of declining profit margins by paying abysmally low wages and obliging the workers to undertake unpaid overtime work. Indeed, cheap, skilled and docile labour is the main source of competitive advantage of such suppliers in large retailer-driven global commodity chains.

Jatindra Nath Saikia (2010), explained that the Assam Government has to try hard to bring weaving to such an extent that our past glory and reputation in weaving would be appreciated again in the world. Assam should try its level best to regain our past golden history of weaving by producing the best quality fabrics which can complete in the international market. The department of Handloom and Textile, Assam and weaving cooperative societies working under this department can take major imitative bringing back the pride, glory and reputation. In order to achieve these objectives the handloom and textile sector of Assam requires a booster dose from the Government.

Kusugal (2010), in his study concluded that the occupational shift of women towards rural non-farm sector was mainly driven by the poverty distress related factors, whereas in respect of males, it was determined by growth related factors originating from agriculture. A shift of workers away from agriculture in favour of the rural non-farm sector tends to raise the wage rates of the existing labourers in agriculture and thereby contributing to a decline in poverty. Occupational diversification in favour of RNF, therefore, has dual impact, direct and indirect, on reduction of poverty. It can be concluded that in view of a gradual decline in the share of the Government expenditure for rural development and poverty alleviation programmes, the promotion of RNF followed by agricultural growth and human resource development can be considered as an important policy intervention to tackle the long-standing problem of poverty in rural areas.

Shyamala and Haridoss (2010), in their article remarked that in India, social, assistance is meager, and social insurance is limited and fragmentary, in both cases. It mainly covers BPL person rather that all unorganized sector worker house holds. Only one third of the latter are in the BPL category, two – thirds of them are above the poverty line. However, as the NCEUS has argued, on the basis of National sample survey, 2004-05, on Employment, 77 per cent of the house holds in the country live on an amount of less than Rs.20. Therefore, the case is strong for both increasing social assistance for unorganized sector workers, and for introducing social insurance. Nevertheless, it remains to be seen how much political commitment there really is to actually implement these things even for all BPL workers in the unorganized sector, let alone for unorganized workers who are above the poverty line.

Brajesh Jha (2011) adopted a diagnostic to approach problems of non-farm employment in rural sector and identified by studying pattern and process of rural employment using data from the NSS quinquennial survey results on employment, unorganized manufacturing and also the CSO Economic Census results. Preliminary analysis showed that the share of non-farm sector in the rural workforce has increased significantly in the recent period. Productive employment in the rural sector however remains important. The share of women in the rural workforce has increased significantly, but one-third of rural female workers employed on the basis of usual status are actually unemployed on the basis of current daily status of employment. The study further investigates pattern of rural diversification using a mix of data for aggregate and disaggregate levels. The findings suggest an increased importance of distress-related factors in rural diversification. In the development-induced rural diversification though agriculture is important; analysis of different sets of data suggests that the role of agriculture in rural diversification is decreasing over the years. Alternate drivers of rural diversification have significant implications for employment, poverty and inequity of the region. The study finds that agriculture, manufacturing and tourism are the engines of rural growth; and development-induced rural diversification in a region warrants growth in one of the above engines. The growth of manufacturing in particular is important. In spite of numerous public institutions to encourage manufacturing and business in rural sector; productivity of rural manufacturing remains low, flight of primary-resource based manufacturing to urban sector continues. The paper therefore argues for different kind of incentives to encourage manufacturing in rural vicinity. A single window integrated service centre to promote rural non farm sector is also important; in this regard Rural Non-farm Development Agency (RNDA) of Rajasthan provides an example.

Anu Muhammad (2011) in her paper reveals that Bangladesh's ready-made garments industry has taken the low road to competitive advantage. Local capitalists, the big retailers and western governments are reaping the benefits of the super-exploitation and repression of the (mostly women) workers. Inevitably, the resistance of the victims is taking shape.

Women Workers in Match Industries

Vina Mazumdar (1975) in her article "Women workers in changing Economy" states that in the traditional economy women have played integral and protected roles in agriculture, industry, and services. Development with increasing complexity of markets, production techniques and technological changes have been the relentless force which has displaced large masses of working women from their traditional occupations, made their productive and professional skills obsolete, and reduced them to the status of unskilled unwanted workers. The alternative opportunities that have opened up as a result of development in services on new industry are for a different class of women educated and with new type of skills. They cannot absorb the displaced women who are mostly illiterate, rural and with restricted mobility.

Perumalammal (1981) in her study titled "Women workers of match factories in Thayilpatti, Kamarajar District" has analyzed the working and living conditions of women workers in match industry. The study is based on 56 match industries of Kamarajar District. The researcher observed that the working conditions of women workers of the industry taken up for study were unsatisfactory because they were oppressed with long hours of work, low wages, and poor heath and the like.

Ramalakshmi (1982) in her study titled "An economic study of the working and living conditions of the women labour in the match units in Virudhunagar" had tried to bring out the importance of the working and living conditions of the women labourers in the units where men and children were also working. She found that the match industry was highly labour intensive and women were given only piece wages. The findings also revealed that the work is suitable only as a secondary or supplementary one, but was primary for the women. Mostly men are not willing to take up such jobs. According to this study, women are working due to poor economic conditions and a considerable portion of the income is spent on bare necessities.

Moulik and Purushotham (1982) in their study titled "A study of match industry in Sivakasi" indicates the various findings, which include women members supervising all operations performed by hired labourers. The wage payment is followed and they are paid on piece rate basis. They work more than 9 hours in the factory and on returning to their homes they do spend another three or four hours in box making. This shows how hard they worked to get more wages to meet their family expenditure.

Usha Rao (1983) in her study deals with the all India pattern of varied types of women workers. For her, there has been a growing concern in recent years regarding the declining work participation rates of women in India. Regarding the services sector it may be mentioned that according to the occupational categories of the census, there has been a marginal increase in the proportion of women in white collared occupations, viz, doctors, nurses and other heath personnel, teachers, clerical staff and office workers. This increase has been offset by the decline in the number of women in trade, commerce and other categories. This expression requires a lot of in depth secondary data analysis.

A study was conducted by Smith Kothari (1983) to know the working conditions of women workers of match industry in Sivakasi. According to him, the working conditions of women workers in match industry are poor. Three is very little facility for ventilation in the small rooms of the cottage units. Similarly all the activities require squatting, which makes the women uncomfortable and forces them to suffer from postural defect. The occupational conditions in the various production stages are hazardous.

Natararajn (1987) in his study titled "The wage problems of women and child workers in the safety match industry" observed that the child and women labourers are getting low wages and that there is discrimination in the wages between these two and of the men workers. He gives the following reasons for such wage differences.

1. The contribution of labour in safety matches is heterogeneous in character.
2. A dominating feature of child labour and women workers.
3. Lack of capital and creditworthiness along with market imperfections and uncertainty.
4. Lack of workers associations and ignorance of labour legislations. He suggested that the steps have to be taken to protect the child labour and the women workers from being exploited by restricting working hours and fixing minimum wages. Proper implementation of the Harban Singh Committee Report (on child labour) should be insisted on. The government should provide easy and cheap credit facilities.

Gomathi (1988) in her study titled "A study of job satisfaction of women employees in public and private sector banks in Tirunelveli Town" has analyzed the theme of job satisfaction. She has found that the employees of public sectors are highly satisfied than those in private sectors.

Kathiresan (1989) conducted a study titled "Perception towards specific aspects of the work situation". He has examined the extent of satisfaction or dissatisfaction on job factors, as perceived by workers and trade union leaders. For the conduct of the study, the dispute prone textile units were identified and then, a total of 708 workers and 67 trade union leaders were contacted, from the units thus identified at random. Most satisfactory factors are perceived by the workers are supervision and opportunity for advancement. Though the workers perceive leave facilities, working conditions, termination policy and hours of work as satisfactory, the extent of satisfaction is very low. Trade union leaders perceive supervision and leave facilities as the most satisfactory ones as compared to other job factors. However, they consider opportunity of advancement, working conditions and hours of work as the most satisfactory ones.

Gopalsamy (1989) in his research work titled "A study of human resources in Ramnad District central co-operative bank in Madurai" has studied the various aspects of the personnel management situations prevailing in the bank. He observed that the employees are recruited mainly from district employment office and the promotion policies adopted by the bank do no give satisfaction to the employees of the bank.

Kaptan (1990) in one article "A case study of Amaravathi city: The Income, wages and working conditions of women workers in the unorganized sector" explains that insecurity and uncertainty, heavy burden, stagnant wages, long working hours and temporary nature of work were found in the occupational structure of unorganized women working as beedi makers, cotton spinners, tea plantation workers, grain mill producers. He has reported that these women may not work after 40 years as they had already lost their physical stamina or working capacity by doing long hours of work.

Narasimhalu and Sathya Murthy (1991) in their study "Performance of Match Industry" a case study of Chitoor district have stated that cottage Match Industry has a unique place since it offers job to male, female and children. Further it does to need huge investment in plant and machinery.

Narasimhalu and Sathya Murthy (1991) in their study "Performance of Match Industry" a case study of Chitoor district have stated that cottage match industry has a unique place since it offers job to male, female and children. Further it does to need huge investment in plant and machinery.

Manim Mekalai and Sundari (1991) studied on, "Female Labour force in the unorganized sector of Mat Industry-Some Evidence", which they carried out in Amoor and Ayyampalayam villages in Tamilnadu. The pathetic condition of women in the unorganized sector is highlighted in that study. These women labourers were forced by poverty and destitution to accept low pay and insecure work in the match industry.

Madasamy (1994) in his unpublished thesis titled "A study on the problems of production in cottage Match industrial units in Kamarajar District" has analyzed the raw materials and labour problems of match units. He has also discussed the sources of working capital and the process of manufacturing. He has suggested that the entrepreneurs should be exempted from getting exemption certificates for cottage match units. He has also disused the sources of working capital and the process of manufacturing. He has suggested that the entrepreneurs should be exempted from getting exemption certificates for cottage match units. He has also suggested that the licenses issued for chemicals like chloride and sulphur should be for at least three years. In order to provide more employment opportunity he has suggested that the government should encourage entrepreneurs to start cottage match units. He also suggested that the procedure for getting the subsidiary and term loans should be simplified.

Mehra (1994) in his study, "The working conditions of women workers in informal sector" has indicated that self-employed women in unorganized sector being poor are exploited and are low class workers. Labour laws and other special benefits which are available to women workers in organized sector are not available for informal sector.

Subhara Patwa (1995) in his study "The comparative study of female and male workers in diamond trade industry" indicated that female labour receives less awards than males. It had been revealed that advantage to industry is more from female labour on account of characteristics of female labour such as reliability. The strict gender specific literacy at firm level does not accept females as brokers or co-merchants and at and manufacturing level where male worker would not like to take orders from female managers. Owners curtail self-employment opportunities for females. The study cautions that any deliberate attempt to undertake feminization of manufacturing units will the female more vulnerable in terms of lower wages.

Janette Moritz (1995) who carried out research in Ahamedabad city of Gujarat state on "women workers in the waste Economy", explains that collaboration with the self-employed women's Association (SEWA) focused on the employment experiences of twenty five paper pickers in the city. This study also brought out the hardships of women in the form of exploit in, lack of protection and infrastructural support, job insecurity and absence of organized power for collective bargaining. Eighty-eight percent of the participants started working between the ages of twelve and fifteen and some as young as at nine years of age in agricultural and factory work, domestic service and waste collection.

The study on the living conditions of workers in Bakery industry in India[18] (1995) revealed that 95 percent of the total workers in the industries were men, 4percent women and only one percent children. The percentage of scheduled caste and scheduled tribe workers was only 1.77 and 0.17 respectively. 59 percent of the workers were unskilled, 17 percent semiskilled and 24 percent skilled. 66 percent of the workers were male and 34 percent female. About 32 percent of the units were extending maternity benefits to the female employees and Employees State Insurance Act 98 percent of the units were provided with drinking water facility.

Ganiger *et al*., (1996) in this work "The study on female employment in non-agricultural sector in urban Karnataka" reveals that urban work participation rate in non-agricultural sector in Karnataka has not depicted significant increase during 1977, 1991 and has remained very low. This study has witnessed gradual replacement of male workers by female workers in professions like teaching, purse making and beedi making. The study has enlisted reasons that prevented women from choosing modern occupations, like low level of literacy, lack of proper skill, absence of competition avenues, etc.

Tripathy *et al*., (1996) found most of the women labourers in the unorganized sector without fair wages and good living standards and invisible vulnerability. Treated as second class citizens women workers are putting in more hours of work than men and yet without participation in the decision making process.

Preethi Rustogi (1997) states that the level of female participation in the unorganized sector tremendously increasing due to economic compulsion, low employment, avenues, increasing cost of living and employer's preference.

Saraswathy (1999) in her paper "Women labour in unorganized sector needs reappraisal of labour laws" explains that while women's issues in the developed world are more sharply focused on the equality question, in the developing countries, these issues are seen primarily as developmental. This is not to imply that equality is not an issue for the developing countries. However, the present development crisis and controversies about the impact of development on women's employment conditions have pushed the question in the background. These issues have been discussed in her paper.

Harbans Singh (1999), in the study, the researcher analyses the impact of the rural labourers were defined as change in soico-economic conditions and changes in employment income and socio economic status. This study was undertaken in the nonagricultural labourers in Chandigar. A sample of 150 respondents was selected by random sampling for the purpose of the study. A structural interview schedule was prepared and collected by conducting personal interview with the 150 respondents. He pointed out that the problems of the nonagricultural labourers in Chandigar are lack of job availability, lack of awareness level about the governmental labour laws, and backwardness in education.

Amarjothi (2000) explained the human resource management of match industry in Sivakasi. It was found that about 76 percent girls and 24 percent of boys were engaged in this match industry. The cause for the employment of more number of female child labourers is the preference by employees to female children. In these match industries the contribution of child labourers to their families is sizeable. In total an average of 22 percent of the total family income is contributed by the children who have substantially increased the income level of the households of the working children.

Amarjothi (2000) explained the human resource management of match industry in Sivakasi. It was found that about 76 percent girls and 24 percent of boys were engaged in this match industry. The cause for the employment of more number of female child labourers is the preference by employers to female children. In these match industries the contribution of child labourers to their families is sizeable. In total an average of 22 percent of the total family income is contributed by the child which has substantially increased the income level of the households of the working children.

Ramana Rao (2001) studied the impact of institutional credit on the socio- economic conditions of rural women in self-help groups. From this analysis, it is obvious that the Self-Help Groups have spread their reach by serving a large client with small amount of credit, but financial re-opening of credit system through Self-Help Group movement still remains a far cry. Further there seems to be a tendency among Self-Help Groups members to borrow from various agencies, which may lead to repayment problems due to multiple financing. In this connection, the policy to integrate Self-help Group within mainstream banking should receive greater attention. Only 24 percent of Self-Help Groups members demanded credit for agricultural purpose and in terms of amount also it constituted a big chunk (24 percent) of the total demand for credit.

Rajasekhar *et al.*, (2006) in their article remarked that the role of trade unions in helping women beedi workers to obtain statutory benefits has been analysed in this paper with the help of data collected from 28 trade unions and 876 beedi workers from four Karnataka districts. It is shown that in the context of growing unorganised component within the beedi industry and limited membership base, trade unions find it difficult to organise women workers to access statutory benefits although they have fairly good understanding of the situation and needs of the workers. An important finding is that production relations emerging within the industry explain whether a worker is able to access the benefits or not. It is argued that when workers are being increasingly unorganised, the role of trade unions in ensuring that there is collective bargaining of the workers will become either marginal or non-existent as trade unions find it difficult to change the strategies in view of changing conditions.

Women Workers in Brick Industry

Singh (1981) explained that a vast majority of the countrys is workforce is in the unorganised sector, and consequently unprotected. In the absence of economic opportunities where they live, many migrate across the states of India to seek casual employment. Brick production depends almost entirely on migrant workers, half of whom are women. This paper looks into the socio-economic status of women workers in the brick industry of Haryana and underlines the fact that these workers have a very tough life. While bearing and rearing children remains their primary responsibility, they are invariably involved in economic activities for survival, thus playing roles in both production and reproduction.

Guerin Isabelle *et al.* (1981) shows that workers are in a "mild" situation of debt bondage, have to work for long hours, and very often put their children to work as well. However, they are paid wages that are very close to the rates fixed by the government and the system of advance payment is endorsed by both workers and kiln owners and the former see it as a means to social mobility. Only the coming together of employers, unions, NGOs, public authorities and job brokers can help to break the debt bondage.

While studying the economic bondage of brick kiln workers of Muzaffar nagar district in Uttar Pradesh, Chopra (1982) found that the majority of the labourers were from the Scheduled Castes, of whom over 75 percentage were illiterate. Out of the sample of 340, only 69 workers reported having rebelled against their bondage. These workers were then forced by the kiln owners to remain on the site either to perform household duties in their homes or to do agricultural work. The study showed that 45 per cent of the total numbers of workers were women. Working hours were extremely long, none of the respondents reporting less than 12 hours a day, 40.4 percentage said they worked between 12 and 18 hours a day, while 54.3 percentage worked between 18 and 22 hours a day; 78.8 percentage of these workers were in debt.

The surveys of the Labour Bureau (Government of India 1988b) in the north Indian states of Punjab and Haryana found that women workers employed in brick kilns were mostly migrant labourers from areas within as well as outside these states. Women constituted nearly 44 per cent of the total workforce in the kilns, nearly 94 per cent of them working as helpers to moulders or loaders/unloaders. Women were not found doing work like digging earth, transporting mud and preparing the mud mixture for moulding, these tasks were carried out only by men. Brick kilns have no fixed working hours and usually the work is spread over 11 to 12 hours a day. It was noticed that almost 98.5 per cent of women workers and more than half the children did not attend school. Not a single male or female worker was reported to be a member of a trade union. No woman worker was aware of the beneficial provisions of various labour legislations. Most of the women resided in temporary hutments which were erected in and around the kilns with material supplied by employers. There were no facilities such as separate kitchens, bathrooms, lavatories and creches.

Dharmalingam (1995) found that brick workers in a village in Tamil Nadu were underpaid, with no hope of a better future. Only 6 per cent of the main workers and 4 per cent of their co-workers/ helpers were more than 40 years of age. About 60 per cent of the main workers had worked for more than 10 years. While some of the co-workers were under 15 years, all the main workers were over 15. The main workers had no connection with the employer, but only with a contractor. Co-workers were always under the control of the main workers. The wage of the main worker was determined by the number of bricks made, but the wage of the coworker was fixed by the main worker on the basis of capacity. If rain destroyed the bricks laid out, then the main worker had to forgo his wage as well as that of his co-worker. Over 70 per cent of the main workers were in debt. The accident most often experienced in brick kilns was injury to the foot, a hazard occurring when mixing the mud mixture with a spade. An additional occupational hazard was exposure to heat and dust.

According to Gulati (1997) who analysed through a case study the work and family life of women in the brick industry, there is a rigid compartmentalization of work on the basis of sex. Women are employed exclusively for carrying head loads, while all skilled and semi-skilled work such as moulding, shaping and stacking is done by men only. As a result, women's wages, for work which is not physically less exhausting than men's, are only about half the wages earned by men. Nevertheless, women cling to the brick industry because of uncertain work opportunities elsewhere and the continuity of employment that this industry offers. After 20 years, Gulati revisited the Scheduled Caste woman whom she had studied earlier to investigate any change that might have taken place. Sadly, she found the women were in dire straits in all respects (Gulati and Gulati 1997). Therefore, on the whole, it appears from existing data that workers in brick production, including women, are highly exploited.

Using the 1978-88 National sample survey data Srinivasa Rao (2000) has tried to examine factors determining the rural non-farm employment through regression analysis. Person day unemployment rate in agricultural sector is positively and significantly related with rural non-farm employment according to this study, besides agricultural Sector, he has conducted the same exercises for rural non-farm employment in manufacturing and service sectors too. The finding of his study reveals the fact that the agricultural development has no influence on the share of these sectors to total rural non-farm employment bust only the person day unemployment has a positive and significant influence on these sectors.

Samal C.Kishor (2000) has conducted a study on the determinants of rural non-farm employment in Orissa. Unfavorable conditions in rural areas such a prevalence of capitalist production in agriculture, decline of handicrafts, inadequate income, poverty, unemployment, under-employment, seasonal employment, loss of poverty and sources of income due to natural calamities etc., pushed the landless agricultural labourers out of agricultural occupation and they are forced to search for jobs in the informal sector. According to his findings, the literacy rate in Orissa is positively influenced by the level of urbanization and negatively by poverty. Literacy level and education help in increasing the productivity and skill of workers. Which in turn mostly stimulate the growth of modern informal rural sector with new technology.

Singh (2002) in his article remarked that a vast majority of the country's workforce is in the unorganised sector, and consequently unprotected. In the absence of economic opportunities where they live, many migrate across the states of India to seek casual employment. Brick production depends almost entirely on migrant workers, half of whom are women. This paper looks into the socio-economic status of women workers in the brick industry of Haryana and underlines the fact that these workers have a very tough life. While bearing and rearing children remains their primary responsibility, they are invariably involved in economic activities for survival, thus playing roles in both production and reproduction.

Iain Stuart (2005) in the context of renewed interest in artefact analysis in Australian historical archaeology, this paper discusses the methods and attributes that have been used to analyse bricks in the past, and concludes by suggesting a standard set of attributes for future analysis.

Amal Mandal (2010) in his paper remarked that economic compulsions coerce the vast majority of poor women workers to perform strenuous manual labour for survival. This is a report on the conditions that are debasing and discriminatory of women workers in brick production.

Women Workers in Construction Work

In the communist manifesto, the origin of trade unions (1952) is described thus: with the development of the industry, the proletariat not only increases in number, it becomes concentrated in greater masses, its strength grows, and it feels that strength more... the collisions between individual workmen and individual bourgeois take more and more the character of collisions between two classes. There upon the workers begin to form combinations (trade unions) against bourgeois; they club together in order to keep up the rate of wages; they found permanent associations in order to make provision before hand for these occasional revolts.

Another pre-independent report was the "Report of the Labour Investigation committee" brought out in 1946. This report was an improvement over that published in 1931. Details of wages paid and the terms of employment were selectively analyzed by it. However the working conditions, wage differentials were not sufficiently dealt with. The acts of identification and assessment of total number of construction workers in India found some importance. Market imperfections, wage fixations trends and existence of exploitation were not adequately discussed by this report. As a systematic second report it drew attention from labour managers and some industrialist.

An Adhoc Survey (1954) of labour conditions was conducted by the labour Bureau of the Government of India in 1954. In that survey the nature and the growth of the building and construction industry were analyzed clearly.

The labour Bureau conducted a Comprehensive Survey during 1957-61. The problems of contract labour and their wage levels were the central points of discussion in that survey. However such attempts were made at the macro levels and did not give much importance to the minute micro details.

Pandey and Vikram (1960) came out with an article titled "Trade Unions in Delhi's Building Industry". They have explained the salient aspects of Trade Unionism in Building

Industry in Delhi. In their study a brief description of the building industry and its work force was give as the general background which is necessary for understanding the salient aspects of unionization in this industry.

The International Labour Organisation (ILO) published a "Report of the Building, Civil Engineering and Public Works Committee" in 1964. It was concerned mainly on migration and other basic problems. The problems of seasonal workers were also studied. It was felt then that the scope of this exercise could have been wider with a perspective projection.

Sylos-Labini Paola (1964) suggests that the concept of precarious employment may be of developing countries and regions than the usual concepts of open unemployment disguised unemployment and under employment. According to the author a large part of total employment is precarious in a backward economy. It implies the absence of any guarantee o stability either of job or income.

Pant (1965) has studied Indian labour problems and published them in 1965. In that he has examined the extent and types of differences in wages among several sectors of the labour market. His inter industry and intra-industry comparisons are valuable to draw meaningful inferences and logical conclusions as far as wage differentials are concerned. This study gains added importance in the light of the fact no such scrutiny was commonly made earlier. His findings and recommendations have served remarkably in the formulation and reformulation of policies relating to working hours, wage payments and rate of exploitation found in the labour market.

A study on seasonal unemployment was made by Jan Witt rock in 1967. The title was "Reducing Seasonal Unemployment in the construction Industry-Methods of stabilizing construction Activity and Employee Income". The author presents a brilliant discussion of the structure of the industry, seasonal pattern of unemployment, the benefits of eliminating seasonal fluctuations, the technical aspects of winter construction and the pattern of remuneration to labourers. A number of recommendations were also made for the betterment of construction workers. The author has proposed suitable training courses for the potential job seekers.

In a combined study, Pandey and Johri (1970) have investigated the management o construction labour in selected chemical plants in India in the year 1970. Their main analysis was about workers engaged in the organized sector and also about the legislative protections available for construction labourers and the cases violations and abuses.

As outstanding study were Employment, Incomes and Equality: A strategy for productive Employment in Kenya" (1972). In the study the frustration of unemployed job seekers, poverty level and low productivity were analyzed. The several possible solutions also were offered. The report dealt with the then prevailing situation in the construction sector and made suitable recommendations for the future. It was a pioneering study with economic importance, and social relevance.

Again, Pandey and Johri (1972) had undertaken a study on the employment relationship in the building industry in Delhi in 1972. The National Building Organization had sponsored that study. It was mainly about the employment of workers in the building industry in and around New Delhi. The nature of employment in the building industry, labour supply, their mobility income, debt conditions and the issues relating to the recruitment, working conditions and training of construction labourers were studied by them.

Giri (1972) the former President of India was a Champion of trade-unionism and labour welfare. He had undertaken many studies of immense value and wisdom carefully. His excellent theoretical understanding coupled with empirical evidences were inherent in his studies and reports which won him reputed status literature relating to labour problems, policies and welfare. A noteworthy publication came from his masterly pen in 1972 entitled "Labour Problems in Indian

Industray". In his outstanding work he has evaluated the efficiency of trade union efforts and bi-lateral agreement as prevailed in countries like Great Britain, France, the Netherlands, Belgium, Newzeland, Australia, Canada and India. The study was path-breaking in the sense that it was almost a pioneering comment on contemporary conflicts and harmonies relating to the labour. It paved the way for further exploration of knowledge in this direction.

Another interesting study was on "Labour Conditions and Industrial Relations of the Building industry in Mexico conducted by Dmitri and Gemidion", (1974). This study has analysed the role of labour in building industry, the relation between the social partners in the industry and the labour market in the building industry. A realistic approach to the question of labour problems also is made. A. qualitative analysis of labour in the building sector is made with a touch of thoroughness. The theoretical frame work offered by this study seems to be highly useful for future investigations.

Bose and Swadesh (1975) studied the problems of the construction workers under the title some aspects of unskilled labour markets for civil constructions in India: observations based on field investigations". The above paper represented the first attempt in India at examining the aspect of substitution of labour and equipment in civil construction. Civil construction is highly seasonal in character. The problems of migrant labour are also studied. Investigations were held in Madhya Pradesh and also in Tamil Nadu.

Sinha and Renade (1975) in their article "Women construction workers" one in India covering nine construction sites, covering two major Government Projects. This study was about the socio-demographic characteristics of women workers, the system of recruitment, working conditions, type of work and wage rates, heath status, living and welfare facilities. It is also about the women workers in the organized construction sector and it deals with non compliance of welfare measures. This study identical the exploitation of construction workers.

Subramanian, Veena and Parikh (1979) in their article on "construction labour market at Ahmadabad". This study covers 64 construction work sites and 1000 workers. This study analyzed details of various types of construction activities, categories of workers employed and their socio-economic characteristics, earnings and conditions of work and levels of living. It also reveals that more than 50 per cent of the workers are in the organized sector receiving monthly wages. It analyses explains the abuses in the wage payment.

Palvia and Jeganathan (1978) made a study of the problems of employment of building construction labour in Kaval towns of Utter Pradesh. It was an effective socio-economic survey of the working and living conditions of labour in the building sector. They have analyzed the labour problems, the format of low co-operation and welfare laws of workers.

Guha Thakurta (1980) has undertaken a study of contract labour in construction industry at Tripura in 1980. The main concentration of the study was mostly on the condition of employment, wage determinant in un-organised sector, low welfare and social security measures. The scope of this study was confined just to construction workers. The problem of non-implementations of welfare measures by the construction agencies was reported.

Another remarkable study was made by Stretton (1981) - "The Construction Industry and Urbanisation in Third World Country-A Philippine Case Study". A model constructing of the structure of the industry the migrates nature of works and skill formation any construction labourers was built. In the study, the nature of employment in the building industry was aptly highlighted. A few hypotheses were also tested brilliantly.

Ravindran Nair (1990) explained that in the Informal Sector one of the most exploited groups are the women Construction workers. They suffer from temporary and shifting nature of work and undergo enormous physical strain, toiling hard in all seasons. And also, they are suffering from insecurity exploitation by the contractors and middlemen. Frequent changes in their work sties and the uncertain nature of their work deprive them and their children of the basic needs like health, education. Employers seldom pay them wages on time; the payments remain unsettled even when the women are leaving the work site for their native places.

While considering the above mentioned studies it becomes clear that the unorganized rural labour constitutes a major chunk of the agricultural sector, which has the largest work forces in the country. Since they are unorganized, they are vulnerable to all kinds of exploitation. By and large, they are not represented by major trade union, union, though in the past two decades, a number of organizations including registered trade unions and voluntary organization have been making efforts to organize them.

Tripathy (1996) in his work titled "Women Labour in Construction sector in Orissa" used Data about Women Labour in Construction work. With a view to collection data on the socio economic conditions of women labourers. The peculiarities in the nature of construction work are some of the causes for the unstable relationship between employer and employee, the insecurity of employment, difficulty in enforcing the existing labour laws and regulations related to this industry and the problems encountered while organizing the labour force.

Hariya Priya (1996) concluded that the present study on violence against women construction workers based on a primary survey of 150 women workers from three organizations highlights interesting findings.

Majority of the respondents needs to cover a distance of 5-10 km. to reach their work place. Majority of the workers have an experience of less than five years and only 18.7 per cent has more than 10 years of experience. 42.3 per cent of the respondents joined construction sector due to poverty. Majority of them joined this sector due to circumstantial poverty (husband/parents died) by chance and not by choice.

More than half of the respondents (53.3 %) are illiterate without attending any formal schooling. Being a politically active and aware state, 68 per cent of the respondents are members of construction union affiliated to either ruling left party or opposition party. The union provides variety of welfare activities such as old age pension, crisis support etc. The union also educates its members on entitlement and other rights.

At the same time 28 per cent of the respondents felt that the number of women respondents in the union is inadequate and the existing women members are not pro-active. 24.7 per cent of the respondents have infants and children less than six years of age. The organizations never provide crèche facility and these women are depending on neighbours, parents, in laws etc to look after the infants. 76.6 per cent are unskilled manual labourers.

Majority of the respondents could not attain any skilled job due to family responsibilities, poverty, etc. None of the organizations provides toilet facilities, and these women depend on neighbours' toilets or go to isolated places or bushes for their needs. Abusive tendency of co-workers and sub contractors are the main type of harassment and harassment leads to mental depression, uneasiness and adversely affects the productivity. Respondents did not report rape and molestation cases but many of them have extra marital relations with co-workers and sub contractors/contractors, Most of them have only emotional attachment because 36 per cent of the respondent's husbands are alcoholic and 30 per cent are wife beaters.

Lalitha (1999) in her paper, "Female labour force in construction industry" explains that working conditions and occupational hazards are inseparable. In the organized sector, a significant percentage of women are engaged in construction industry. The number of women workers in construction industry has increased from 2.9 lakhs in 1951 to 7 lakhs in 1991 in India. The condition of women construction workers is pitiable. They face instability and insecurity of employment are paid low wages, are not protected by labour laws and are even exploited by middlemen who employ them without providing adequate facilities and securities enjoined by legislation. Their life is perceptually in a state of flux as they have to keep on migrating from site to site. The average wages for women are generally lower than that of their male counterparts. Further, women construction workers are totally unskilled. In the event of accidents, sickness or during maternity, workers had to forgo employment and wages. They were in debt during the crisis periods either to the money lenders, neighbours or to subcontractors. The study undertaken at Athoor block of Dindigul District revealed that 76 percent of the women construction workers expressed willingness to become skilled. Therefore, workers special efforts should be made for imparting skill training like masonry and carpentry to women workers under government and Non-Government organization initiatives. There should be a statutory provision for contribution by the contractors to the extent of 10 percent of net earnings towards construction workers welfare fund.

Jeet Sing Mann (2000) in his work titled "Welfare and Protective Measures Pertaining to the Construction Workers in India", mentions that normally constructions are employed through contractors, who exploit them for their benefits. Though there are various protective enactments for these workers, but in practice this is totally opposite. Contractors employ these workers till they remain capable of performing the assign tasks. Whenever they fall sick or become disabled, they are thrown out of the employment without any social security benefits as specified under the building and other construction workers (Regulations of Employment and Conduct of Service, Act, 1996 or Contract Labour Act, 1970). Workers are unorganized and incapable to bargain on the issue of welfare and social protection. Moreover there is no single agency which ensures the effective and efficient implementation of relevant schemes. It is the need of the hour to formulate a comprehensive protection law covering all construction workers for all adversities, not only at work place but also afterward. The proposed scheme is equipped with single enforcement mechanism. The success of any scheme depends upon its implementation. Otherwise the legislation remains a piece of paper for workers.

Self Employed Women's Association (2000) expressed their view that construction workers are the largest group of service providers in Ahmadabad city. SEWA has been organizing workers in the dyeing, the chemical and the screen-printing industry for many years now. However, in recent years, major changes have occurred in these industries due to rapid mechanization. As an outcome of industrialization, unemployment is rampant and women workers have turned to construction as an alternative source of income generation. SEWA is now actively organizing these women. There are more than 5,00,000 women workers engaged in the construction industry in Gujarat. What is their socio-economic status and how do they manage to earn their daily livelihood? What are the problems faced by these construction workers and what are their demands? How to bring them into the mainstream of the construction sector and provide them with recognition from the authorities? These are some of the issues which need to be addressed immediately.

Sreeja (2003), in her article "on Environmental and Occupational Hazards of women Construction Workers in selected village of Agasteeswaram Taluk" mentioned that the educated, trained and skilled women labour force could compete on par with the male labour to take advantage of lucrative job opportunities offered by liberalization and globalization. On the other hand, the uneducated, unskilled and untrained women labour could not find jobs opportunities in construction activities, modern activities and so on. It is found that liberalization has caused an increasing inequality in employment opportunities and incomes. Economic opportunities created by the upper income, upper skill end, the quality as well as opportunities or employment have improved for most women workers however, the quality of employment is poor, without opportunities for employment and income of women workers are examined, four distinct trends are visible (i) lose of existing employment without creation of new employment (ii) changes due to new technologies and skills (iii) information of work and (iv) creation of new employment opportunities.

Ram Lakhani (2004) in his study has undertaken to assess the occupational health status of women workers in the construction industry by evaluating incidences of occupational health disorders. One thousand and fifty-two workers were selected by stratified random sampling, medically examined and subject to relevant interviews, examinations and investigations. Over three-fourths of the women and almost all men reported working for 10 to 12 hours daily. A majority of the women were reported to have headaches and backaches, as well as pain in the limbs. Fifty-six per cent of women and 16 per cent of men reported injuries resulting in work loss. They had no social security or other workers' benefits. Most women and men said that they would prefer to do some other work. Respiratory, eye and skin disorders and noise-induced hearing loss (NIHL) were found to be prevalent amongst workers exposed to hazards like dust, noise, heat and cold, non-ionising radiation, and exposure to dry cement, glass and adhesives, tar and paint. About 76 per cent women reported gender-specific work stress factors, such as sex discrimination, and balancing work and family demands, above and beyond the impact of general job stressors such as job overload and skill underutilisation. Discriminatory barriers to financial and career advancement were found to be linked to recurrent physical and psychological symptoms and more frequent visits to the doctor among women workers.

The Construction Industry today is a dynamic, changing work environment that offers excellent career opportunities. Firms all over the world are modernizing, applying new technologies, expanding internationally, and employing more engineers than ever before. Small, medium, and large construction firms alike are striving for the most modern management on their projects and as businesses. By using modern technology and current management methods, constructors are leaving behind the image of the construction workplace as a grimy and labour-intensive setting (Construction Jobs, Manpower from India, Constr.hmt, 2006).

Dileep Kumar (2006) in his study indicates the plight of the construction labourers in Pune, district Maharashtra state. Majority construction labourers migrated from different regions from Maharashtra. The construct ion sites have more than 100 labourers. The living conditions are very poor and the labourers are staying in tin sheeted and rubber sheeted houses. Some construction companies are making provision of accommodation facilities to the labourers, while majority labourers have to build temporary huts by themselves, near by the site.

The construction company is not making provision of any electricity on sanitation facility to the construction labourers. The sanitation hygiene of the construction site and the labourer's houses are found in poor condition. Majority sites do not have any toilets. Where the sites have toilets there it is having substandard quality. There is limited provision of drinking water and the labourers have to depend on bore well, tanker lorry water and public water supply. The construction company is not making provision of water facility for washing clothes and cleaning their utensils. There also the labourers have to depend on open well, public water supply, bore well, etc. Some of the construction companies are not making facility for washing at all. Majority construction site doesn't have any bathroom facility. Labourers have to depend on open bath, from where water is available (Dileep Kumar, Indianmba.com, 2006).

Santhanam (2007) remarked that, shortage of construction workers is slowing down the industrial growth in metros and major cities across the country. The findings of a study on the availability of skilled manpower in various sectors Commissioned by the Confederation of Indian Industry (CII) also confirmed the alarming trend.

Amarathunga (2007) in his article on "Construction Industry and women", mentioned that the UK construction industry has particularly low participation in the UK. However, despite increases in the number of women employed in the construction over the past decade, they still constitute only 9% of the work force. This means that the construction industry will continue to be male dominated. It is found that women are confronted by a significant number of barriers, beginning with difficulties in joining the field of construction through to capturing the most senior position in the organizations hierarchy

Sanghita Bhattachrayya and Kim Korinek (2007) have written the article "Opportunities and vulnerabilities of female Migrants in construction work in India," This paper is based on a case study of female migrants working in construction, the second largest industry in India and one which employs almost 30 million people approximately 30 percent of which are women and many of are them migrants. In this paper, we extend beyond an empirical description of female migrant workers in the field of construction, considering the selective and menaced realities linked to women's lives. experienced as migrants. The study is based on interviews of 110 female construction workers who have migrated from various regions of India to the city of Delhi an in-depth, qualitative exploration of these women's lives and perceptions captures some of the more latent risks and rewards associated with both migration and work in the informal sector. Specifically, the results shed light on how strong societal norms may actually prevent women from acknowledging or articulating the true reasons for their migrations.

Kamalakannan (2007) in his article "Women construction workers in Tamilnadu", has stated that women constitute almost half the population of India and the contribution of this population in the socio-economic development of the country has been vital. Women below poverty line, have to perform demotic duties and also supplement the family income by going to work. Since they are unskilled and illiterate they are subjected to economic exploitation with low and discriminatory wages. Government officials, NGOs and Trade unions should take measures for the well being of women construction workers. In the recent past Self help groups will be formed among construction workers for the economic empowerment.

Devi M. Kamatchi and Jeyanthi (2008) in their article on "women construction workers in Sivakasi" mention that women occupy a disadvantaged position in the society. Most of them are occupied in low category of work, where there is wage discrimination, male domination and many more economic and social problem. In their working places women's rights are violated by the make groups. They do not know their rights in the society and the main reason for that is their illiteracy. By educating them the Government can make them realize their rights in the society. By arranging awareness comps about various organizations, the Government can do remedial actions against violence.

Anjali Alexander (2008) says that construction Workers Welfare Association has funds to the tune of Rs.1.2 billion for the benefit of labourers, but hardly any of it is being used. This is because only one percent of the city's construction workers are registered with the welfare board. Sanjay Kumar of Self Employed Women's Association (SEWA) said that the welfare fund for the construction workers serves no purpose because it doesn't benefit the people who actually need them.

Sinha (2008) talks about the efforts made by the National Academy of Construction at Hyderabad to formalise the training of construction labourers. The construction industry is the second largest employment provider next to agriculture in the Indian economy, employing approximately 3.1 crore workers annually (estimates vary). It is roughly estimated that about 8 per cent of the construction labour in India are from Andhra Pradesh. It supplies labour force not only to its adjoining states, but also to the Middle East.

Khosla (2008) said many Indian construction workers are choosing not to take jobs in Dubai because their earnings would be eroded by the UAE dirham's peg to the tumbling US dollar, Middle East Economic Digest (MEED) reported. South Asian labour, mainly from India, is the backbone of the construction industry in Dubai, which is building palm-tree shaped islands and the world's tallest skyscraper in the $20 billion Burj Dubai development. He also said Indian construction workers would expect to earn four times as much as they would in India if they moved to Dubai five years ago. But as the US currency hits record lows against the euro and a basket of major currencies, the pay difference has been reduced to 40 per cent.

Nuzhat Parveen *et al.*, (2010) in their paper found that workers working in the unorganized sector even though contributing a major share to the national development are unsecured and backward socio-economically, educationally, politically, and in other aspects. Women are playing a dominant role in certain aspects in the informal sector such as agriculture, construction, etc. The present paper discusses on the nature of work of women in the informal sectors and analyzes national level statistics on the informal sector. Further, on the basis of different studies conducted on the women in informal sector and in construction, the present study analyzes the problems of the women construction workers.

Annette Barnabas (2011) in her article found that the construction sector is one of the largest employers of women next to agriculture in India. This article analyses the data from a large sample of men and women construction workers, and proposes ways to empower women workers. Most of them are very poor and destitute, face harassment at both home and workplace and do the heaviest work. This study suggests training for women as masons to equalise their opportunities.

Women Workers in Other Non-farm Workers

Pramod Kumar Bajpai (1990) studied on observed "that the workers in saw mills have to work very hard in handling the huge wood logs which result in rapid heart beating to pump blood leading to high/low blood pressure causing cardio vascular problems"

Manim Mekalai and Sundari (1991) study on, "Female Labour force in the unorganized sector of Mat industry: Some Evidence", which they carried out in Amoor and Ayyampalayam villages in Tamilnadu. The pathetic condition of women in the unorganized sector is highlighted in that study. These women labourers were forced by poverty and destitution to accept low pay and insecure work in the Mat industry.

Mehra (1994) in his study, "The working conditions of women workers in informal sector" has indicated that self employed women in unorganized sector being poor are exploited and are low class workers. Labour laws and other special benefits which are available to women workers in organized sector are not available for informal sector.

Subhadra Patwa (1995) in a study "The comparative study of female and male workers in diamond trade industry" indicated that female labour receives less awards than males. It has been revealed that advantage to industry is more from female labour on account of characteristics of female labour such as reliability. The strict gender specific literacy at firm level does not accept females as brokers or co-merchants and at and manufacturing level where male worker would not like to take orders from female managers. Owners curtail self employment opportunities for females. The study cautions that any deliberate attempt to undertake feminization of manufacturing units will make the female more vulnerable in terms of lower wages.

Janette Moritz (1995) who carried out research in Ahamedabad city of Gujarat state on "Women workers in the waste Economy", explains that collaboration with the Self Employed Women's Association (SEWA) focused on the employment experiences of twenty five paper pickers in the city. This study also brought out the hardships of women in the form of exploitation, lack of protection and infrastructural support, job insecurity and absence of organized power for collective bargaining. Eighty-eight percent of the participants started working between the ages of twelve and fifteen and some as young as at nine years of age in agricultural and factory work, domestic service and waste collection.

The study on living conditions of workers in Bakery industry in India (1995) revealed that 95 percent of the total workers in the industries were men, 4 percent women and only 1 percent children. The percentage of scheduled caste and scheduled tribe workers was only 1.77 and 0.17 respectively. 59 percent of the workers were unskilled, 17 percent semiskilled and 24 percent skilled. 66 percent of the workers were male and 34 percent female. About 32 percent of the units were extending maternity benefits to the female employees and Employees State Insurance Act 98 percent of the units were provided with drinking water facility.

Ganiger and Rajeshwari (1996) in their study "The study on female employment in non-agricultural sector in urban Karnataka" found that urban work participation rate in non-agricultural sector in Karnataka has not depicted significant increase during 1977, 1991 and he remained very low. This study has witnessed gradual replacement of male workers by female workers in professions like teaching, purse making and beedi making. The study has enlisted reasons that prevented women from choosing modern occupations, like low level of literacy, lack of proper skill, absence of competition avenues, etc.

Tripathy and Patnaik (1996) found most of the women labourers in the unorganized sector without fair wages and good living standard and invisible vulnerability. Treated as second class citizens women workers are putting in more hours of work than men and yet without participation in the decision making process.

Preeti Rustagi (1997) states that the level of female participation in the unorganized sector is tremendously increasing due to economic compulsion, low employment, avenues, increasing cost of living and employer's preference.

Meenakshi Sundaram (1999) in his paper "Working Conditions of Women Workers in Tanneries" says that in Tamialnadu leather industry plays a vital role in the process of industrial development. Tamilnadu contributes nearly 55 percent of total leather exported from India. 70 percent of the total hides and skins produced in the country are tanned and finished in Tanneries located in Dindigul. For these Tanneries the labour force is drawn from in and around Dindigul. The study analyzed the working conditions of women employees. The study revealed that, the women labourers were employed on temporary basis as helpers which is mostly considered to be unskilled, wages paid were very low and medical allowance was inadequate and poor transport facilities exist for the workers to reach the tanneries from their village.

Saraswathy (1999) in her paper "Women labour in unorganized sector needs reappraisal of labour laws" explains that while women's issues in the developed world are more sharply focused on the equality question, in the developing countries, these issues are seen primarily as developmental. This is not to imply that equality is not an issue for the developing countries. However, the present development crisis and the controversies about the impact of development on women's employment conditions have pushed the question in the background. These issues have been discussed in her paper.

Harbans Singh (1999), analyses the impact of the rural laboures were defined as change in socio-economic conditions and changes in employment income and socio economic status. This study was undertaken in the non agricultural labourers in Chandigar. A sample of 150 respondents were selected by random sampling for the purpose of the study. A structural interview schedule was prepared and collected by conducting personal interview with the 150 respondents. He pointed out that the problems of the non agricultural labourers in Chandigar are lack of job availability, lack of awareness level about the government labour laws, and backwardness in education.

Reena Jhabvala and Shalint Sinha (2001) in their article named "Social security for women workers", in the unorganized sector indicate the advent of globalization in India has seen an increasing normalization of employment including home based, contract and causal labour. This is the complete absence of any widespread system or social security in this sector.

Singh Mor (2001) in his article on "women and the unorganized sector" explained that there is a felt need to spotlight alteration on the problems of women workers in the unorganized sector. This sector usually escapes the notice of enumerators and policy makers alike. The empowerment of workers in this sector will bring about a quantum changes in the lives of disadvantaged women. The plight of the women in unorganized sector is miserable as they work of extremely low wages, with total lack of join security and unprotected by any government labour legislation.

Vijaya Kumar and Shbhayamma (2001) in their article titled "social security for unorganized sector in India", A need for comprehensive reforms explained that in the wage of globalization process, the Indian economy is experiencing several sectoral and structural changes. The last of providing social security to the proportionately large number of labour force in the unorganized sector is becoming a challenge to the government. Experiences from other countries suggest that the need for reforming the existing age-old social security mechanisms. He presented a critical review of the existing social security system for unorganized sector and suggests certain issues, which need through investigation to form an effective social security policy in India.

Vanamala (2001) has examined the impact of reforms on female workers in the informal segments of an engineering unit. She concludes that traditionally, the wages of female workers have been fixed lower than the male workers in male denominated informal industries. But, the industry does not employ female employees on the management side, not even at the supervisory levels. Women workers are appointed only on the operation side at the tail, end of the production process. And also, she concludes that the working girls recruited are yond and they have to carryout the operation for 8 to 16 hours in a standing position. So, the working conditions in the industry are explorative.

Ramana Rao (2001) studied the impact of institutional credit on the socio-economic conditions of rural women in self help groups. From this analysis, it is obvious that the Self-Help Groups have spread their reach by serving a large client with small amount of credit, but financial de-opening of credit system through Self-Help Group movement still remains a far cry. Further there seems to be tendency among Self-Help Groups members to borrow from various agencies, which may lead to repayment problems due to multiple financing. In this connection, the policy to integrate Self-Help Group within mainstream banking should receive greater attention. Only 24 percent of Self-Help Groups members demanded credit for agricultural purposes and in terms of amount also it constituted a big chunk (24 percent) of the total demand for credit.

Sukit Desgupta (2003) in his article on" Women organizing for socio economic security" explained women workers in the unorganized economy are amongst those with least access to social security. Given their vulnerable status at home and at work, income generation alone may not improve their socio-economic status. Their economic empowerment needs to go alone with political empowerment which could improve their bargaining power both in the household and at work. This means that organizing women workers in the unorganized economy could have beneficial impact on their work and their life.

Mangaiyarkarasi (2003), in her study analyses the work pattern of women industrial workers, their job satisfaction and the problems they face. The women surveyed stated that they preferred this employment because it provided more recognition than domestic work. The rising trend of factory employment for women can be encouraged by giving adequate training opportunities.

Arul Kamaraj and Muralidaran (2005), say that women are considered the human resource of choice for the unorganized sector because they lack education and training and are amenable to accept lower wages for equal work due to gender casting. The role of the voluntary sector in workers education is crucial for determining a better developmental path for the unorganized workers.

Women workers development should be viewed as an issue in social development but also seen as an essential component in every dimension of development. The match industry is considered a vital one in many aspects. It provides major employment opportunities to women in this district. The present study is a novel attempt to study the life style of women workers in match industries. The findings of the present study will be highly useful to the workers chambers and employer of the match association, state and Central Government and employer of the match industries in particular to improve the quality of life of women workers in match industries.

Lalitha (2006) in her paper concluded that one of the challenges of reform is to improve the quality of employment and income in RNFE. The strategy needed for enhancement in the livelihood of rural poor are as follows: government should have policies to improve education and skills of workers. The incomes of women have to be improved by creating opportunities in the higher productivity sectors. Most of the women are confined to agriculture. There was only 0.7 increase in the share of RNFE during the reform period. For the above strategies pro poor growth engines have to be identified at sub sectoral level rather than at the level of broader sectors. Public investment in agriculture and RNFE has to be improved significantly to improve the quality of RNFE. Infrastructure development and other incentives are needed for attracting private investment. The Government has to address policy constraints on raising agricultural production, growth of small and medium business, technological progress improve productivity of natural resources and the marketing of rural products. Allowing the poor to contribute to and benefit from increased growth will pose particular challenges as employment in India is largely in the unorganized sector.

Patel and Reena (2008) in their study viewed that in the past decade, a night shift labour force has gained momentum in the global economy. They hyper growth of the transnational call centre industry in India provides a quintessential example. The night shift requirement of the transnational call industry also intersects with the spatial and temporal construction of gender. Research conducted in 2006 in Mumbai, Bangalore and Ahmadabad indicates that the night scape is primarily a male domain (with the exception of prostitutes, bar dancers, and call girls) and women's entry into their domain generates a range of diverse responses from call centers, their employees, the employees' families, the media, and the Indian Public.

This research illustrates that there is no linear outcome to how working the night shift at a call center affects women's lives. Even though the global nature of the work combined with the relatively high salary is viewed as a liberating force in the lives of workers in actuality women simultaneous experience opening and constriction for working in the industry. Through the collection of interviews, focus group data, and participant observation gathered during 10 months of filed work in India, I examine female night shift workers' physical, temporal, social and economic mobility to illustrate how global night shift labour is intersecting wit the lives of women in ironic and unsettling ways.

Call center employment certainly changes the temporal mobility of some women because it provides them with a legitimate reason to leave the house at night, whereas before this was considered unacceptable. Concerns about promiscuity and "bad character" related to working at night are deflected by linking employment to skill acquisition, high wages and a contribution to the household. Women's safety – a code word for their reputation is preserved by segregating them, via private transport from the other women of the night. Women consequently become more physically and economically mobile, but through the use of what I term mobility. Morality narratives households continue to maintain regimes of surveillance and control over when and how women come and go. Similarly their social mobility is limited by obligations to support family members and conform to generated notions of a woman's place.

Vikkraman and Baskaran (2010) in their study viewed that the informal sector plays a significant role in the economy in terms of employment opportunities and poverty alleviation. This sector generates income -earning opportunities for a large number of people. In India, a large section of the total workforce is still in the informal sector, which contributes a sizeable portion of the country's net domestic product. The unincorporated or non-corporate sector has the largest share of national income, manufacturing activities, services, savings, investment, taxes, credit market, employment, Forex earnings, etc. Yet it is little understood, dismissed as 'un-organized', 'informal' or 'residual' sector. It is important that the nature and role of this sector are explored to see how it impacts the economy.

The non-corporate forms of organizations are major players in such activities as manufacturing, construction, transport, trade, hotels and restaurants, and business and personal services. Terming them as "un-organized" is inappropriate as they are well organized" is inappropriate as they are well organized from the economic and organizational point of view. The informal sector got an inherent ability to adopt the changing economic condition, technological changes and customer perceptions with its inbuilt indigenous management practices.

Prasannaa and Jayanthi (2010) remarked that in recent times, participation of women in the workforce has increased around the world still differences between the situations and opportunities of men and women arise from unequal possibilities of access to employment, income and other economic resources. Gender prejudice is a major factor that prevents women from participating effectively in the labour market. This problem appears to be concentrated in the unorganized sector in India.

Vinish Kathiria, RajeshRaj and Kunal Sen (2010), in their paper analyze the productivity performance of both the organized and unorganized segments of the Indian manufacturing sector using unit level data. Both partial and total factor productivity measures are employed. Our analysis reveals that labour productivity has increased for the organized sector over time, whereas both labour productivity and capital intensity growth have slowed down in the unorganized sector during the period between 2000-01 and 2004-05. The improvement in TFP growth in organized manufacturing in the post 2000 period as compared to the second half of the 1990s across most states in India is heartening as also the fact that output growth was mostly productivity driven in the post reform period. However, the declining TFP and the increasing capital intensity of the unorganized sector are causes of worry and raise several important questions.

Anirban Kundu (2010) in his paper analyses the impacts of agrarian growth and land distribution and of corporate led or supported crop diversification on the rural non-farm sector, in particular, and the informal sector, in general. It shows that the informal sector benefits from agriculture if it is constituted mostly of marginal and small farmers, as they demand a majority of the primary equipments for farming and non-farm business. Moreover, the agricultural growth-induced expansion of the rural non-farm sector is conditional upon the size class of landholdings; it is the marginal holdings that have a prosperity-induced impact on the rural non-farm sector. Next, the paper proposes a distress-led eviction of the petty non-farm sector, which largely depends on traditional farming, as agriculture goes for corporate led or supported crop diversification towards high-value crops. An analysis of informal manufacturing units engaged in the processing of agricultural products reveals the dominance of labour-intensive coarse crops processing firms and thereby questions the view that high value crop cultivation would pave the way for non-farm employment generation in the processing sector. On the other hand, it has been found that the wholesale and retail trade of high-value crops is dotted with micro-entrepreneurs who may not be able to compete with the corporate-driven modern agricultural supply chain. Finally, it is argued that crop diversification may create problems of micro food security for the informal producers.

CONCEPT

"Marketing is the process by which goods and services are exchanged and their value determined in terms of money prices".[1]

Primary whole sale markets are where the bulk of arrivals are from village or village huts. These markets are periodically held either once or twice a week or at longer intervals or on special occasions.

Secondary whole sale markets are called Mandis and Gunjs stretch over a wide area covering from 10 to 20 kilometers. There are about 1700 such markets in the country. In these, the bulk of the arrivals are from other markets.

Terminal markets are those markets in which the produce is either finally to disposed of directly to consumers or processors or assembled for shipment to foreign destinations or for redistribution to surrounding areas.[2]

Village markets are those agricultural markets situated in each village or cluster of small villages, held once or twice a week.

Village traders are the pioneers of middleman community in Agricultural marketing. They link the producers with the market.

Commission agents act as a connecting link between the growers and wholesale merchants or sometimes between the village traders and wholesale merchants. They have established places known as Commission Mandis.

The studies discussed above are related, in one way or other to the present study. However, the present study differs from the study in several respects. It has certain special features which have been discussed in the succeeding section.

The present study gives primary importance to the exploitation of women workers. An attempt has been made to find out the contribution of the women workers to their family income besides analyzing the working and living condition of women workers in readymade garment works.

REFERENCES

1. Duddy and Revzan, "Marketing an Institutional Approach", 2001, p. 6.
2. Mamoria, C.B., "Agricultural Problems of India" Nagpur: Kitab Mahal, 1982, pp. 736-738.

Socio-Demographic Characteristics of Women Workers

GENERAL

This section deals with the analysis of data collected with records of the socio-demographic characteristics of women workers in readymade Garment making in Puthiamputhur. It also analyses occupational problems and prospects of women workers in Readymade Garment work.

A sample survey of 1,000 families of the women workers in readymade garment works in the study area was conducted during the period, December 2010 to April 2011. For the study purpose, an interview schedule was designed and used for data collection.

The social characteristics of women workers in readymade garment works families are revealed by the various sizes of households and its compositions in terms of age, religion, community, family size, education, marital status, nature of work are discussed.

RESPONDENTS BY AGE

Women workers work in readymade garment works is a strained and hard work and heavy man power and good physical stamina are indispensable to do this work. As such it would be difficult for one to take up this occupation either in the very early age or continue this occupation after forty years. The respondents covered in different age given in the following table.

Table 3.1

Respondents by Age

Age (in years)	No. of Respondents	Percentage
Up to 15	36	3.60
15-25	354	35 40
25-35	361	36.10
35-45	223	22.30
45-55	15	1.50
55-65	11	1.10
Total	**1,000**	**100.00**

It is evident from the above table that a majority of the sample belongs to the age group of 25-35. The next age group is 15-25 and 35-45 years.

It is known that, about one-third of the workers are under the age group of 25-35 years and another one-third of the respondents are under the age group of 15-25 years. One-fourth of the respondents are under the age group of 35-45 years.

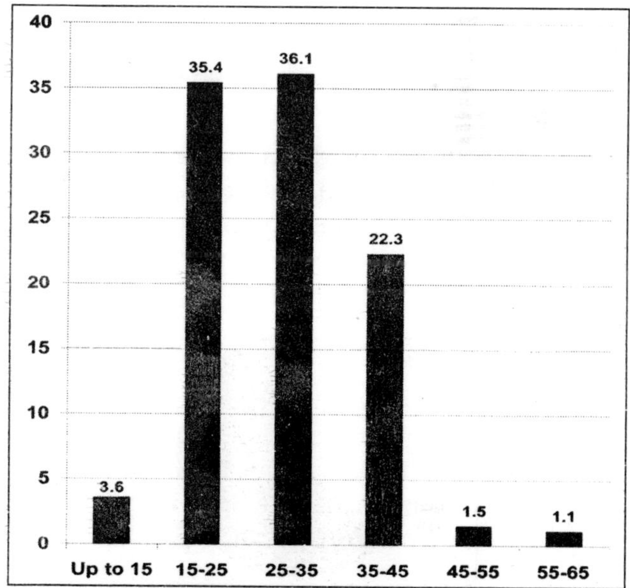

Fig. 3.1: Respondents by Age

RESPONDNETS BY COMMUNITY

Economic development depends upon many factors like family system, caste system and religious dogmas. Of them caste system determines socio- economic conditions of readymade workers in the rural setup. In the study area, majority of the respondents are backward community. All community people are not involved in this work. The following table explains the respondents by community.

Table 3.2

Respondents by Community

Community	No. of Respondents	Percentage
FC	12	1.20
BC	612	61.20
MBC	126	12.60
SC	239	23.90
ST	11	1.10
Total	**1000**	**100.00**

The above table shows that majority of the sample that is 61.20 percentage belongs to BC community, 12.60 percentage belongs to MBC community and 23.90 percentage belong to Schedule Caste community.

Majority of the respondents are backward community. One-seventh of the respondents belong to most backward community and one-fourth of the respondents are from the schedule community.

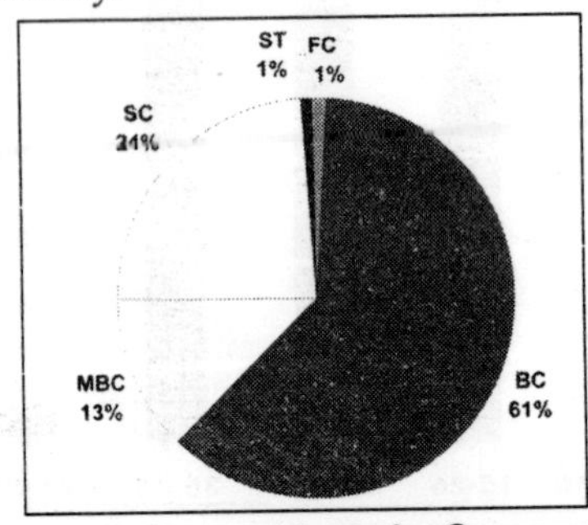

Fig. 3.2: Respondents by Community

RESPONDENTS BY RELIGION

Religion in the Indian society plays a major role in the economic activities especially of women. People belonging to some religion are more conservative and restrict women, particularly unmarried girls, in the rural areas from spending their time outside their houses doing remunerative activities. Religion gives less inducement to the virtues of thrift and hard work and thereby hinders development.

Table 3.3

Respondents by Religion

Religion	No. of Respondents	Percentage
Hindu	817	81.70
Muslim	12	1.20
Christian	171	17.10
Total	**1000**	**100.00**

The above table shows that majority of the sample are Hindus, 17.10 percentage are Christians and 1.20 percentage are Islam. But there is no diversity between the followers of these three religious groups. There exists marital relationship among these religious groups.

Four-fifth of the respondents are Hindus, one-fifth of the respondents are Christians and a meager percentage of the respondents are Islam.

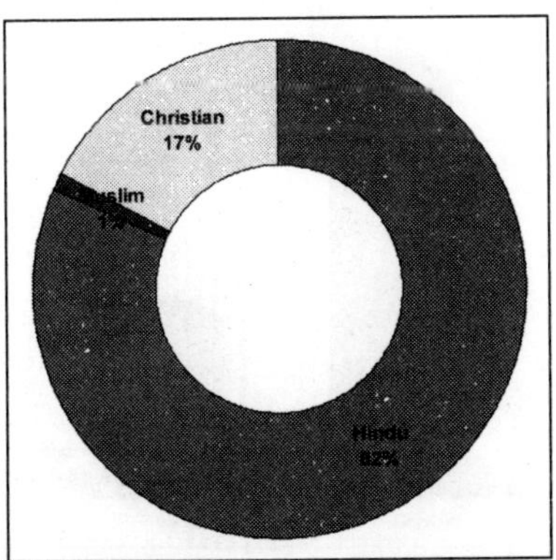

Fig. 3.3: Respondents by Religion

RESPONDENTS BY MARITAL STATUS

Readymade garments workers may also depend upon marital status. Married women with children enjoy a better status in the family than others. In recent times, there has been a trend towards nuclear families, which means that the young married women are no longer under the direct control of their in-laws. At the same time, they confine themselves only to domestic activities and in many cases they are not involved in any income-earning activities. Hence an attempt is made to classify the sample respondents based upon their marital status. The following Table depicts the marital status of the respondents.

Table 3.4

Respondents by Marital Status

Marital Status	No. of Respondents	Percentage
Married	543	54.30
Unmarried	457	45.70
Total	**1000**	**100.00**

The above Table reveals that 54.30 percentage of the total samples are married and 45.70 percentage are unmarried.

It is known that, about one-half of the respondents are married and another one-half of the respondents are unmarried.

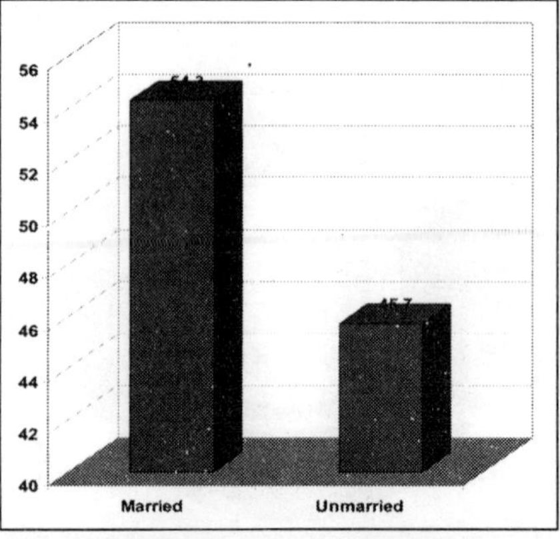

Fig. 3.4: Respondents by Marital Status

RESPONDENTS BY EDUCATIONAL STATUS

In the past, many women workers were against educating their children, since they thought that it would result in independence and a high expectation about life. But this attitude is now changed and most parents like their children to get educated–partly because noon meals are served in schools and partly because educated children have some importance in their villages. The educational status of the sample households is depicted in the following Table.

Table 3.5

Respondents by Educational Status

Educational Status	No. of Respondents	Percentage
Illiterate	64	6.40
Elementary	348	34.80
Middle	337	33.70
Secondary	123	12.30
Higher Secondary	116	11.60
College	12	1.20
Total	1000	100.00

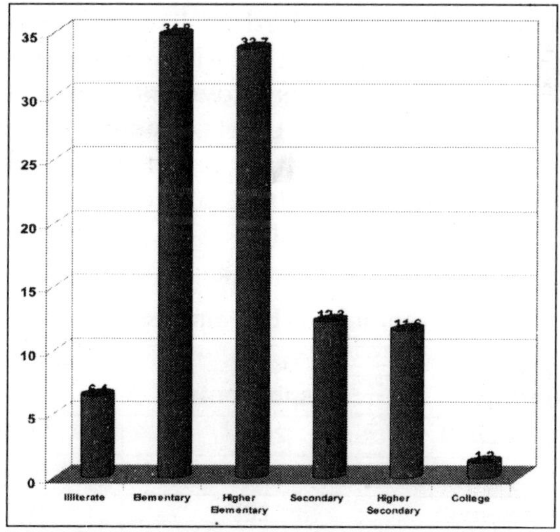

Fig. 3.5: Respondents by Educational Status

From the above table it is clear that, more than 93 per cent of the respondent are literates. It is a peculiar situation in this study area that all have positive attitude towards education. Only 6.4 percentage of the respondents are illiterates they also try to educate their children to the extent possible.

Majority of the women readymade garments workers have studied up to primary level. About one-third of the respondents have studied up to middle level education and about one-seventh of the respondents have studied upto secondary level education. One-fifteenth of the women workers are illiterates and a few of them have studied degree level.

RESPONDENTS BY FAMILY SIZE

The size of the family is an important factor, which determines the economic condition and standard of living of the women readymade garments workers family. If there is more number of young or unemployed members in the family, the income of the family does not increase correspondingly, but contrarily, the expenditure of their family increases. In women workers rural household, larger the size of the family, lower would be the standard of living. However, this proposition may not hold good if the household owns garment industry and has alternative employment during off seasons. Also, the size of the family exerts influence on childcare, recreation, nutrition, education and family welfare. The distribution of sample on the basis of the size of the family is depicted in the following Table.

Table 3.6

Respondents by Family Size

Family Size (in Person)	No. of Respondents	Percentage
Small (Below 3)	206	20.60
Medium (4-6)	674	67.40
Large (Above 6)	120	12.00
Total	**1000**	**100.00**

Among the 1000 sample, 206 sample households have small families, which constitute of below 3 members, 674 households fall in the family size of 4 to 6 members and 120 households have a family size above 6 members.

One-fifth of the respondents' families have up to 3 members i.e small sized family, two-third has 4-6 members i.e., medium sized family and one-seventh have above 6 members i.e., large sized family.

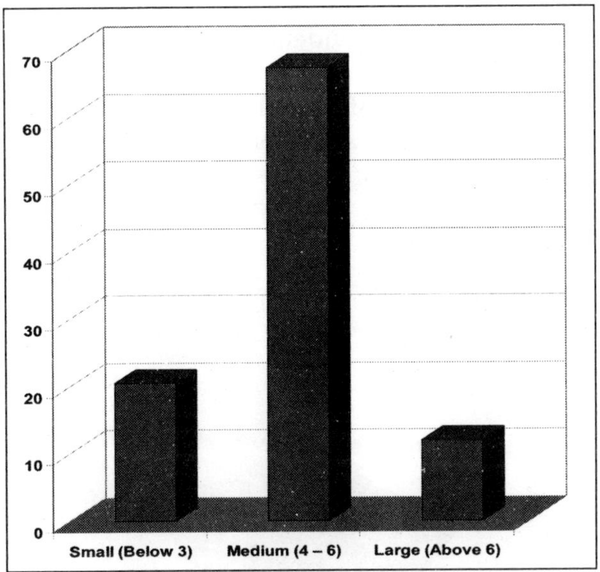

Fig. 3.6: Respondents by Family Size

RESPONDENTS BY EXPERIENCE

The readymade garment workers are found to do the work from childhood. The service of the workers in the readymade garment works is presented in the following table.

The table 3.7 reveals that 41.60 percentage of the respondents are in the service for upto five years, 25.30 percentage of the respondents are with 5-10 years of service, 19.70 percentage of the readymade workers have experience in the readymade works with 10-15 years and the remaining 13.40 percentage of them are with more than 15 years of service.

Table 3.7

Respondents by Experience

Experience (in Years)	No. of Respondents	Percentage
Upto 5 yrs	416	41.60
5-10 yrs	253	25.30
10-15 yrs	197	19.70
Above 15 yrs	134	13.40
Total	**1000**	**100.00**

A majority of the respondents are in the service for five years, one-fourth of the respondents are in the service between 5-10 years, one-fifth of the respondents are in the service between 10-15 years and one-seventh of them are in the service above 15 years.

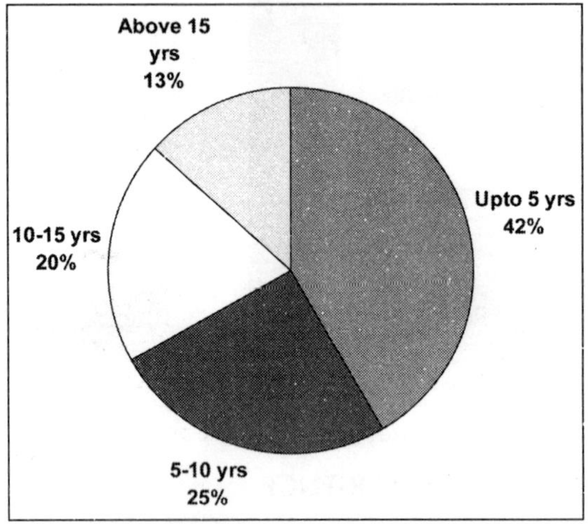

Fig. 3.7: Respondents by Experience

NATURE OF THE WORK

The process of readymade dress making includes cutting, stitching, embroidery, button holing, zip fixing and button sewing. The different stages in dress making done by the women workers are presented in the following Table.

Table 3.8

Respondents by their Nature of Work

Nature of Work	No. of Respondents	Percentage
Cutting	108	10.80
Stitching	608	60.80
Embroidery	74	7.40
Button Holing	108	10.80
Zip Fixing	31	3.10
Button Sewing	71	7.10
Total	**1000**	**100.00**

The above table explains that 60.80 percentage of the respondents are doing stitching work, 10.80 percentage of the respondents are doing cutting the cloths and another 10.80 percentage of the respondents are doing button holing. 7.40 percentage of the workers doing embroidery work, 7.10 percentage of the respondents doing button sewing and the remaining 3.10 percentage of the women workers doing zip fixing.

A majority of the readymade women workers are doing stitching work. One-tenth of the workers doing cloth cutting and another one-tenth women workers are doing button holing and few of them doing other works like embroidery, button sewing and zip fixing.

Income and Savings Pattern of Women Workers

In this chapter, monthly income of the women readymade workers, savings, debts, reasons for joining this work, job satisfaction and other benefits are discussed.

WAGES

The term wage may be defined as a sum of money paid under contract by an employer to a service rendered. The wage policy in all countries is a complex and sensitive area of public policy; because the relative status of workers in the society, their morale and motivation towards productivity, their living standard and infact, their way of life are all conditioned by wages[3].

Methods of Wage Payment

Generally there are three methods of wage payment.

1. Time wages
2. Piece rate wage and
3. Contract rate wages

Under the time wage system a definite sum is paid for a fixed period of time, say an hour, day, week or month. Each worker in a particular category receives the same payment, irrespective of difference in individual output.

Under piece rate wage system, payment of wage depends upon the output turned out by the workers multiplied by the prescribed wage rate. Wages are paid according to the quantity of work done by the worker irrespective of the time he or she takes. Workers in the same category of work may receive different earnings according to the quantity of product produced. That is, one who produces more receives more wages without reference to the different level of ability or those who perform the work.

Under contract system, wages are paid on the basis of an agreement or contract reached between the employer and the worker for a specified work done.

Mode of Wage Payment

Wages are paid to their assistants on the following basis:

1. Time rate
2. Piece rate

In the study area wages are paid in both time and piece rate. The table 4.1 and figure 4.1 reveal the basis of wage payment.

Table 4.1

Mode of Wage Payment

Type of Wage	No. of Respondent	Percentage
Time Rate	520	52.00
Piece Rate	480	48.00
Total	**1000**	**100.00**

The table 4.1 shows that, out of the 1000 respondents, 52 percentage of the respondents are paid time rate and the remaining 48 percentage of the respondents are paid the piece rate.

A majority of the readymade women workers are paid time rate wage and one-fifth of the workers are paid piece rate wage.

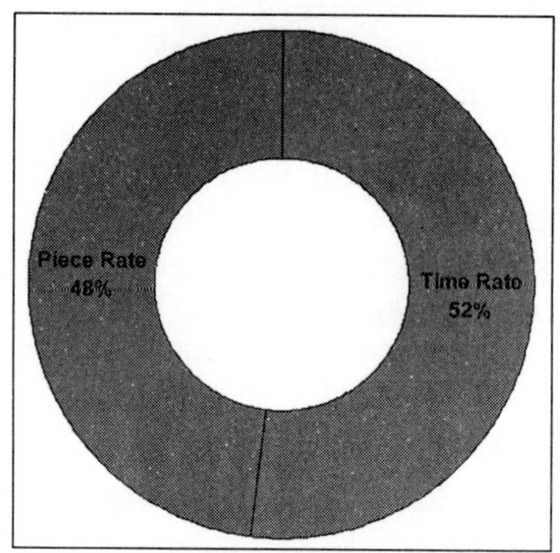

Fig. 4.1: Mode of Wage Payment

GROUPING OF WOMEN WORKERS

Distribution of women workers with respect to income groups is presented in the following table. The women workers are grouped under four income categories according to their monthly income.

Table 4.2

Women Workers by Monthly Income

Monthly Income (in Rs.)	No. of Respondents	Percentage
Below 3,000	135	13.50
3,000-6,000	515	51.50
6,000-9,000	235	23.50
Above 9,000	115	11.50
Total	**1000**	**100.00**

A perusal of the table reveals that a majority of the households are poor in the size class of Rs. 3,000 to 6,000. Out of total, 23.50 percentage of the respondents are earning income between Rs. 6,000 and 9,000. The low income group constitutes 13.50 percentage and the higher income group constitutes only 11.50 percentage.

Hence, from the data collected, it can be inferred that one-half of the respondents earn Rs. 3,000 to 6,000 per month; one-fourth of the respondents earn between Rs. 6,000 and 9,000; one-seventh of the respondents earn below Rs. 3,000 per month and one-tenth of the respondents earn above Rs. 9,000 per month.

Income inequality among the four groups of workers was examined by taking the annual total income of the workers. A Lorenz Curve was drawn to find out the degree of inequality in the distribution of income. The Lorenz Curve is presented in the following figure.

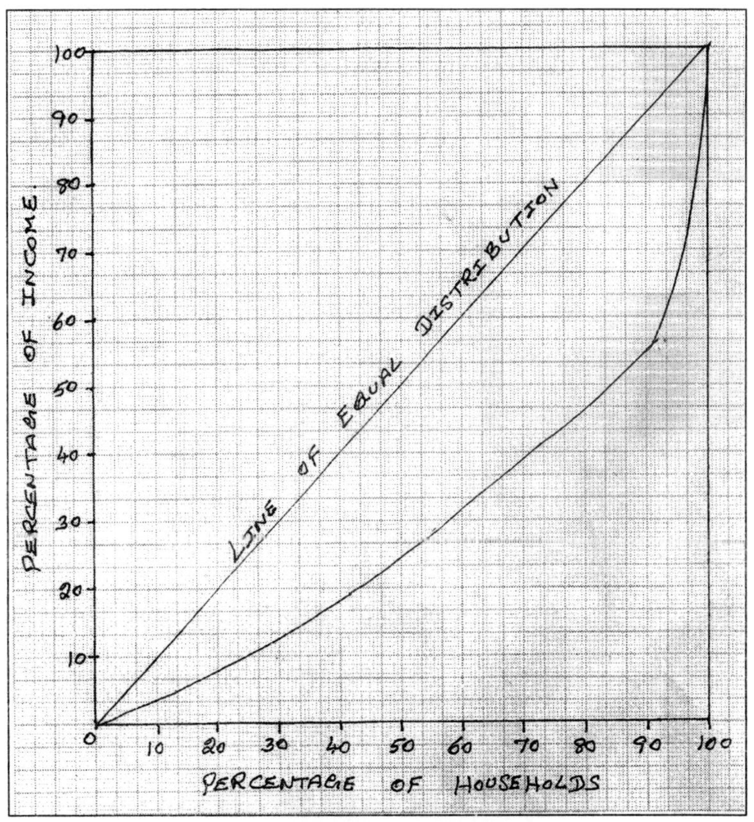

Fig. 4.2: Lorenz Curve – Respondents by Women Workers Monthly Income

Hence it is understood that the curve is away to line of equal distribution. This implies that the inequality income among the four groups of women workers is low. As the graphical representation gives only a rough idea about the inequality, Gini Concentration Ratio was also computed.

GINI CONCENTRATION RATIO

In order to find out the accurate estimation, Gini concentration ratio was calculated as given below:

The Gini coefficient is stated as

$$G = 1 - \Sigma p_i (Z_i + Z_{i-1})$$

where

P_i = cumulative percentage of person

Z_i = cumulative percentage of income

The Gini concentration of this characteristic is 0.2324. This reveals that the degree of inequality is low ie, 0.23. On the whole, the data imply that the income distribution among the four groups of households show a level of low variation.

RELATIONSHIP BETWEEN AGE AND INCOME

Results

The researcher has used the statistical tool 'χ^2' test to study the relationship between income and age group.

Table 4.3

Results of χ^2 Value among Age and Income

Hypothesis (Ho): There is no significant difference between the level of age and income.

Test used: χ^2 test

	Calculated χ^2	Table Value
Age and Income	43.339	26.296

Result: Significant at 5% level

Inference: The calculated χ^2 value is greater than the critical value at 5 percent level. Therefore the Null hypothesis is rejected.

The test employed affirms that there is a significant difference in the level of age and income. Therefore, the first hypothesis as read 'There is no significant difference between the level of age and income' is disproved.

ANNUAL HOUSEHOLD INCOME

The level of income is an important element as it determines mostly the standard of living, saving and investment. Income incured from tailoring generally depends on three factors, viz. the nature of work, number of workers in a family and number of readymade cloth under tailoring. Depending on these inconsistent conditions the income of respondents differs from each other. The classification of respondents on the basis of income from women worker family is illustrated in table 4.4.

Table 4.4

Annual Household Income of Respondents

Annual Household Income (in Rs.)	No. of Respondents	Percentage
Below 25,000	220	22.00
25,000-50,000	360	36.00
50,000-75,000	140	14.00
75,000-1,00,000	180	18.00
Above 1,00,000	100	10.00
Total	**1000**	**100.00**

It is observed from table 4.4 that 22 percentage of the respondents earn an annual income upto Rs. 25,000; 36 percentage earn Rs. 25,000 to 50,000; 14 percentage earn Rs. 50,000 to 75,000; 18 percentage earn Rs. 75,000 to 1,00,000 and 10 percentage earn above Rs. 1,00,000. Majority of the respondents earn an annual income of Rs. 25,000 to 50,000.

Hence, it is concluded that about one-fourth of them are earning a sum below Rs. 25,000; another one-third of them are earning between Rs. 25,000 and 50,000; about one-seventh of them are earning between Rs. 50,000 and 75,000; about one-fifths of them are earning between Rs. 75,000 and 1,00,000 and one-tenth of them earn above Rs. 1,00,000 per year.

EXPENDITURE PATTERN

There is a tendency among the low-income group of women workers family unit to spend a greater part of their income on food, social functions and religious festivals. Therefore, an attempt has been made to find out the expenditure pattern of the women workers in the study area. The total expenditure incurred by the respondents is classified as on food, clothing, fuel and lighting, medicine, education, religious and social functions, entertainment and other expenses which include electricity, telephone, water bills, house maintenance and rent. The end result is depicted in the following table.

Table 4.5

Descriptive Analysis of Annual Expenditure Pattern

Expenditure Pattern	N	Minimum Rs.	Maximum Rs.	Mean Rs.	Standard Deviation	Percentage
Food	1000	24,000	77,000	68,739.75	6,729.35	58.47
Clothing	1000	6,750	35,125	11,332.80	4,231.05	9.64
Fuel & Lighting	1000	1,200	10,750	8,095.00	3,160.90	6.89
Medicine	1000	1,000	4,000	3,031.30	1,947.25	2.58
Education	1000	1,345	13,780	6,841.60	1,140.60	5.82
Religious & Social	1000	940	12,000	8,340.80	748.90	7.09
Entertainment	1000	4,320	19,750	5,842.75	1,175.70	4.97
Others	1000	1,155	9,900	5,341.15	446.05	4.54
Total	**1000**	**40,710**	**72,922**	**47,026.06**	**8,732.36**	**100.00**

On an average, every readymade women worker's family spends about Rs. 47,000 on household expenses. The average amount spent on food is more - about Rs. 68,739.75 ie. 58.47 percentage. They also spend a reasonable sum on education and entertainment, which comes to about 5.82 percentage and 4.97 percentage respectively, and followed by expenditure on social and religious festivals which accounts to be about 7.09 percentage.

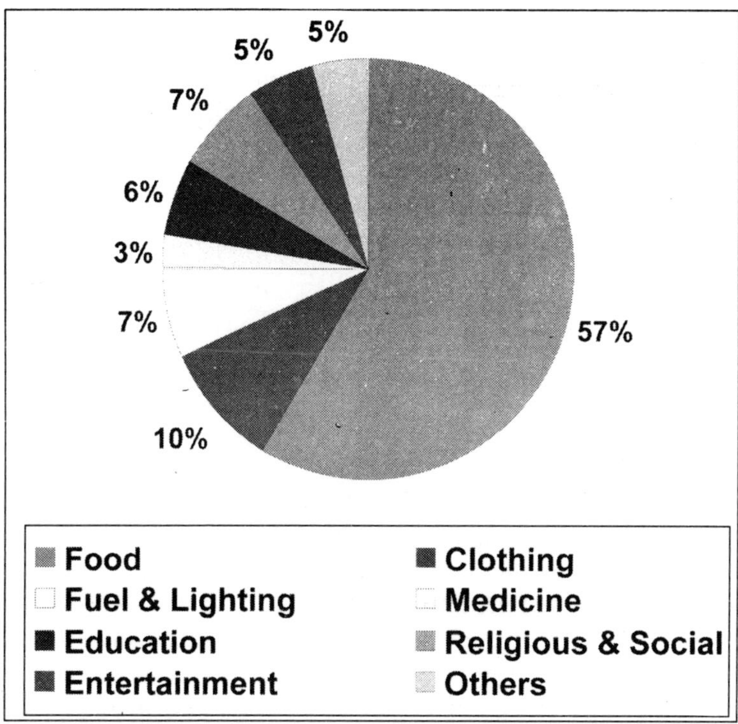

Fig. 4.3: Expenditure Pattern

Hence, it is concluded that majority of the total income is spent on food items. One-tenth of the total income is spent on clothes; another one-tenth of the total income is spent on religious and social functions; One-twentieth of the total income is spent on fuel and lighting; another one-twentieth of the total income is spent on education and a little portion of the total income is spent on medicine, entertainment and others.

ESTIMATION OF TOTAL EXPENDITURE

The total expenditure of readymade women workers' households in Thoothukudi district is regressed upon many interdependent variables. For the present work, three variables were selected viz. family size, family income and amount borrowing by their families. The results of the estimated multiple regression is given in the following table.

Table 4.6

Multiple Linear Regression – estimation of Total Expenditure

	Unstandardized Coefficients B	Std. Error	Standardized Coefficients Beta	t	Sig.
(Constant)	681.381	185.730	0.023	3.333	.598
TOINCOME	0.721	2.088	0.023	1.528	.000
FSIZE	12.678	22.146	0.286	6.449	.000
BORROW	0.286	.022	0.163	3.721	.000
$R^2 = 0.582$		F = 29.524			

Dependent Variable: Total Expenditure

TOINCOME – Total Income; FSIZE - Family Size; BORROW - Borrowings

It has been found that the multiple regression is significant in terms of its 'F' value which is calculated to be 29.524 with an R^2 value of 0.582 explaining nearly 58 per cent of the variations in the family expenditure of women workers. All the co-efficients are found significant at 5 percent level except the constant term. According to the estimated model, the total expenditure increases by Rs. 12.68 for every one unit of increase in the family size. For one rupee of increase in the family income the total expenditure increases by 72 paise. Every one-rupee increase in the amount of borrowing increases the family's expenditure by nearly 29 paise.

ANNUAL SAVINGS

An attempt is made in this section to discuss the savings of the sample households in the selected district Thoothukudi. Savings means, the part of the income remaining after consumption. Saving in undertaken mainly for the sake of security for future to fulfill the future needs and thereby to enhance the standard of living. Even though the women workers' families are greatly in debt, they are prepared to save a small amount. The details regarding the savings pattern are given in table 4.7.

Table 4.7
Annual Saving

Annual Saving	No. of Respondents	Percentage
Upto Rs. 5,000	340	34.00
Rs. 5,000 – 10,000	298	29.80
Rs. 10,000 – 15,000	160	16.00
Above Rs. 15,000	120	12.00
No Saving	82	8.20
Total	**1,000**	**100.00**

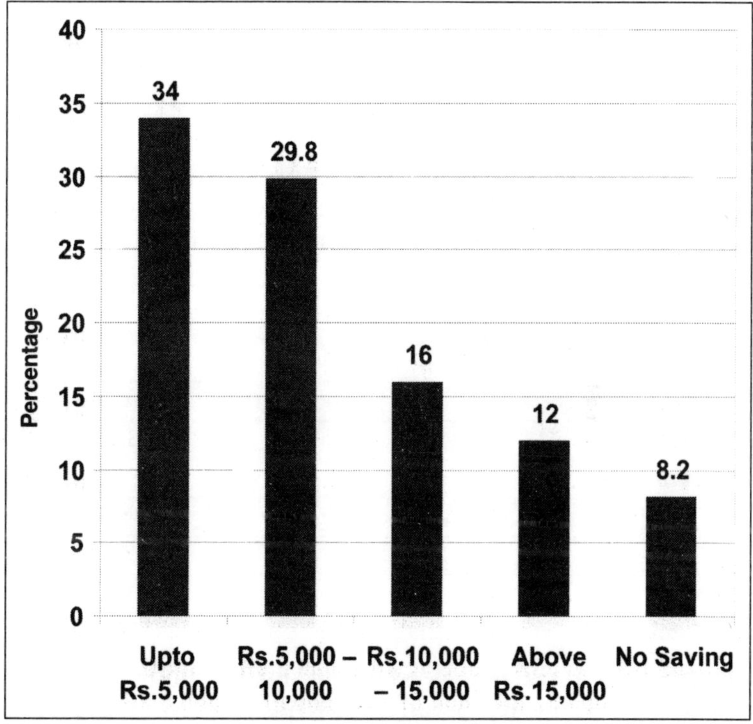

Fig. 4.4: Annual Savings

Most of the women workers (34%) save up to Rs. 3,000 per year; 29.80 percentage save Rs. 5,000 to 10,000 per annum; 16 percentage of the respondents save Rs. 10,000 to 15,000 and the rest save above Rs. 15,000 per annum. A total of 82 women workers has no savings at all. The saving pattern is not very encouraging and it gives the picture of low level of income and low standards of living of the households in the study area.

Majority of the women workers save up to Rs. 3,000 per year and one-third of the respondents save Rs. 5,000 to 10,000 per annum, one-seventh of the respondents save Rs. 10,000 to 15,000 and one-tenth of the respondents save above Rs. 15,000 per annum. One-tenth of the women workers have no savings at all.

MODE OF SAVINGS

The details regarding the savings pattern are given in Table 4.8. Corresponding diagram is given in figure 4.5. From the table it is clear that, most of them are saving in post office and chit funds.

Table 4.8

Mode of Savings

Mode of Savings	No. of Respondents	Percentage
Post Office	84	8.40
Bank	211	21.10
Chit fund	369	36.90
LIC	254	25.40
No Saving	82	8.20
Total	**1000**	**100.00**

A majority of one-third of the respondents save their money in chit funds; One-tenth of the respondents save in post office; One-fifth of the respondents save in bank; one-fourth of the workers save their money in LIC. One-tenth of the respondents have no savings at all.

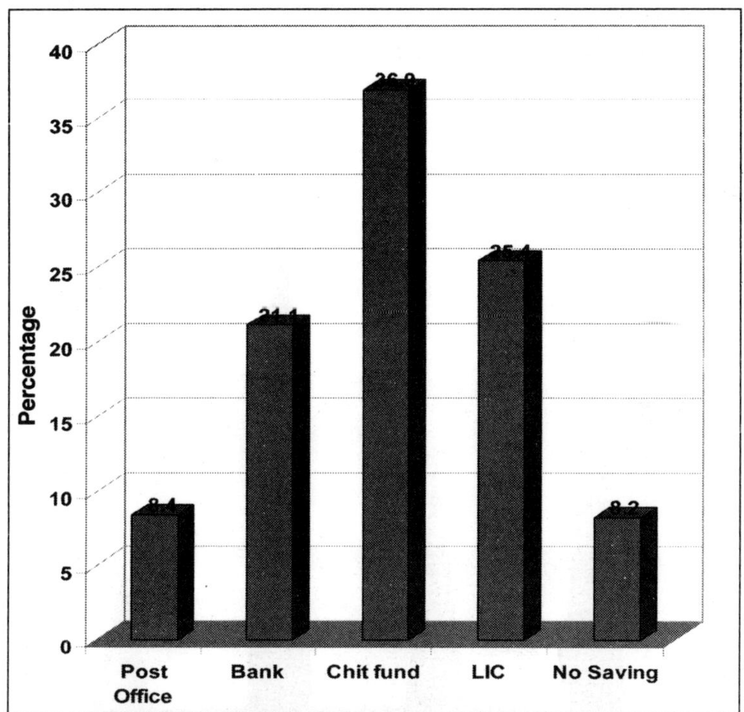

Fig. 4.5: Mode of Savings

INDEBTEDNESS

The amount of debt of readymade garments women workers is given in table 4.9. Most of the loan amounts (42.49%) taken by the readymade garments women workers in the study area are only from self help groups.

Table 4.9

Indebtedness

Source	Amount (in Rs.)	Average	Percentage
Bank	142,000	7,888.89	30.47
Co-operative Bank	80,000	4,210.53	17.17
Self Help Group	198,000	4,714.29	42.49
Friends & Relatives	46,000	3,285.71	9.87
Total	**4,66,000**	**5,010.75**	**100.00**

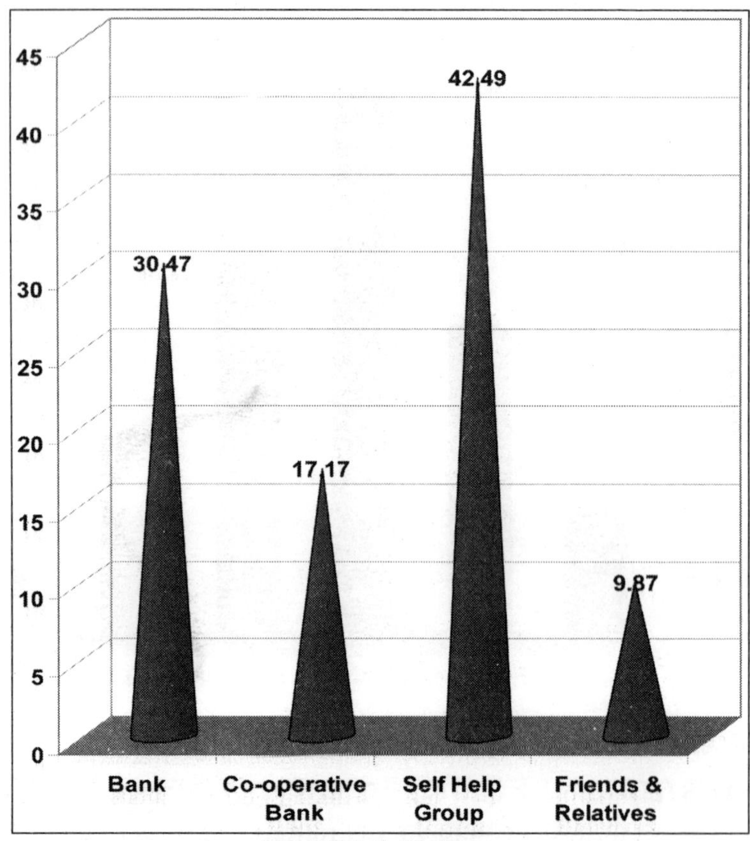

Fig. 4.6: Indebtedness

Most of the loan amounts are availed by the readymade garments women workers only from self help groups. One-fifths of the loans are taken from co-operative bank; another one-fifths of the loan amount is received from self help group and one-tenth of the loan is received from friends and relatives.

DEMAND FACTORS IN WOMEN EMPLOYMENT

The demand factors in the women employment in readymade garments are expressed by workers as classified in the following table.

Table 4.10

Demand Factors in Women Employment

Factors	No. of Respondents	Percentage
Forced by Husband/Father	166	16.60
Better Wages	178	17.80
Easy work	236	23.60
After knowing the backwardness of the family	420	42.00
Total	**1000**	**100.00**

It is clear from the above table that 42 percentage of women readymade workers expressed their readiness understanding the backwardness of their family; 23.60 percentage of them expressed that they opted this job as it is an easy occupation; 17.80 percentage of them expressed that they realized better wages in the industry and the remaining 16.60 percentage of them expressed that they were forced to accept the job by husband and family members. Thus, majority of the women readymade workers expressed that they joined the career knowing the backward condition of their family.

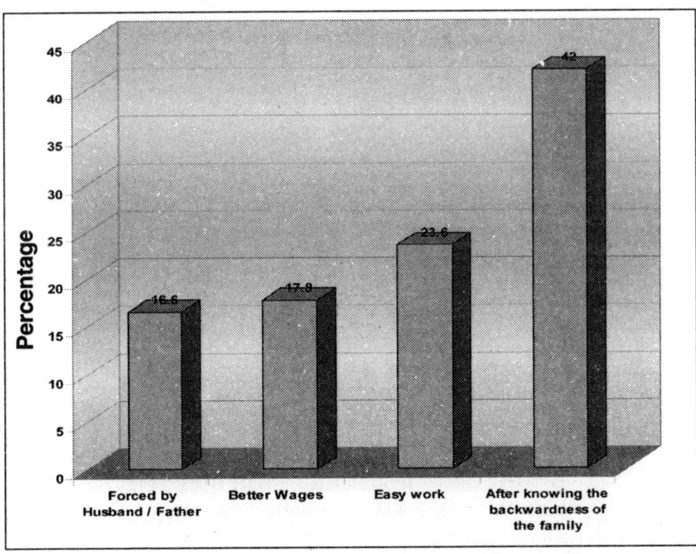

Fig. 4.7: Demand Factors in Women Employment

SUPPLY FACTORS IN WOMEN EMPLOYMENT

The employers of the garment industries also decide the workers to be recruited on the basis of a few criteria. Their experience, age, proper tailoring training, diploma courses etc are considered as the criteria. The following table shows the opinion poll about the supply factor in the women employment in readymade garments work.

Table 4.11

Supply Factors in Women Employment

Factors	No. of Respondents	Percentage
Prior Experience	230	23.00
Proper Training	280	28.00
Diploma Holder	372	37.20
Native Villager	118	11.80
Total	**1000**	**100.00**

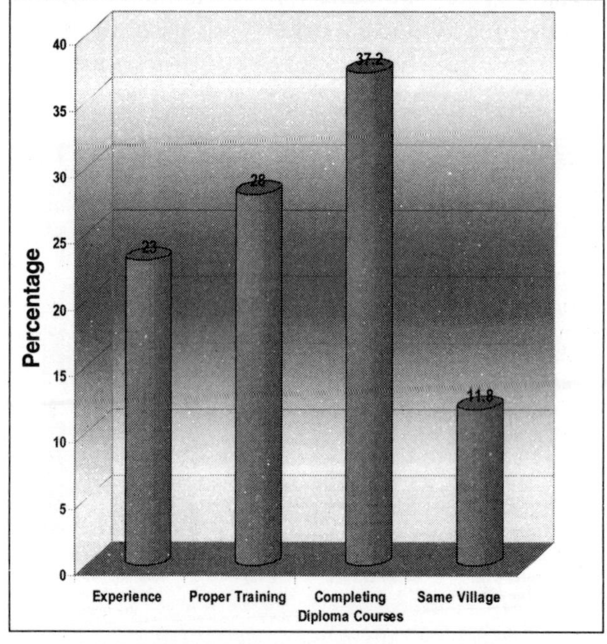

Fig. 4.8: Supply Factors in Women Employment

It is evident from the table that, 37.20 per cent of the respondents have been selected for completing diploma courses. About 280 out of 1000 respondents have been selected for proper training. About 230 out of 1000 respondents have been selected for their experience and about 118 out of 1000 respondents have been selected for their village nativity. As a whole, majority of the respondents have been selected for having completed diploma courses in tailoring.

JOB SATISFACTION

Majority of the respondents are satisfied with the particular job that they undertake. Opinion of the respondents as to whether they are satisfied with the job or not and willing to continue in the same job or prepared to try for other jobs is presented in the following table.

Table 4.12

Job Satisfaction

Job Satisfaction	No. of Respondents	Percentage
Yes	256	25.60
No	744	74.40
Total	1000	100.00

Table 4.12 shows that 25.60 percentage of the respondents show job satisfaction fully and the remaining 74.40 percentage of the respondents are not satisfied with their job.

Thus it is summarized that majority of the women workers of readymade garment works have no job satisfaction and only one-fourth of them are found satisfied with the readymade garment works.

Exploitation of Women Workers

This chapter deals with the working and living conditions and problems faced by women workers of readymade garments and tailoring industry in Thoothukudi district. The investigator personally visited the houses of readymade garments women workers during holidays for having better understanding of the problems being faced such as physical, occupational and psychological problems. During data collection, the investigator felt the unhappy state of affairs prevailed in the tailoring units where the women workers have been working for a long period of years.

Exploitation means 'selfish use of others' property. The Women workers are exploited largely by owners of readymade garment industries. This chapter deals with the problems and exploitation of women workers of readymade garment works.

PROBLEM WITH EMPLOYERS

Employees and employers relationship is very essential in business. Labour relation means relationship between worker and employer. The following table reveals the respondents on the basis of problem with their employers.

The table 5.1 reveals the fact that 10 percentage of the readymade garment women workers face problems with employers regularly and 65 percentage of them face problems by their employers infrequently. Only 25 percentage of the respondents report that they have no problem with their employers.

Table 5.1

Problem formed by Employers

Problems	No. of Respondents	Percentage
Often	100	10.00
Occasionally	650	65.00
No	250	25.00
Total	**1000**	**100.00**

SEXUAL HARASSMENT

One-third of women workers of readymade Garment work are harassed by owners or other men co-workers. It is a main difficulty of readymade garment works.

Table 5.2

Data on Sexual Harassment

Sexual Harassment	No. of Respondents	Percentage
Yes	336	33.60
No	664	66.40
Total	**1000**	**100.00**

From the above table it is found that 66.40 percentage of women workers expressed that they are not affected with sexual harassment and 33.60 percentage of them expressed that they are affected by the sexual harassment by the employers and other men workers.

Hence, majority of the readymade garments women workers expressed that they are not affected by the sexual harassment.

WAGE AND LEAVE PROBLEMS

The readymade garments women workers with multiple responsibilities at home and outside face some wage and leave problems. The problems from the point of view of the women workers engaged in tailoring units in the study area are specified in the following table.

Table 5.3

Nature of Problem

Nature of the Problem	No. of Respondents	Percentage
Wage	663	66.30
Leave	201	20.10
Employer not satisfied with employee's work	102	10.20
Employer not satisfied with employee's behavior	34	3.40
Total	**1000**	**100.00**

The table depicts that majority of the respondents are of the opinion that wage is the most important problem, which constitutes 66.30 percentage, 20.10 percentage of the workers say that leave is another major problem. Out of the total, 10.20 percentage of the respondents say that the employers are not satisfied with their work and 3.40 percentage of respondents express that employers are not satisfied with their behaviour.

A huge majority of the respondents have problems related to wages. One-fifth of the respondents have problems related to leave. One-tenth of the workers are of the opinion that employers are not satisfied with their work. A very few of them opined that employers are not satisfied with their behaviour.

Job Security and Benefits

Every type of business needs to give job security to their workers. If there is no job security, the workersmay not be satisfied with their work and the working environment. The following table reveals job security of respondents.

Table 6.1

Job Security of Respondents

Opinion	No. of Respondents	Percentage
Any time, one may be sent out	250	25.00
As long as one likes to work	260	26.00
As long as readymade works continue	490	49.00
Total	**1000**	**100.00**

The table 6.1 shows the classification of the respondents on the basis of job security; 25 percentage of the respondents say "any time, they may be sent out"; 26 percentage of the respondents say "As long as they like to continue" and 49 percentage of the respondents say "As long as readymade works continue".

It clearly reveals that majority of the women workers say "As long as readymade works continue". One-fourth of the respondents are of the opinion that"as long as they like" and remaining respondents declareuncertainity of their work.

WORK PERIOD AND TIME SPENT

Women workers in readymade garmentworks of the study normally start their work at 9 a.m. everyday. In their working hours they have to work hard without break. The time spent on their work is shown in the following table.

Table 6.2

Time Spent by the Workers

Time Spent	No. of Respondent	Percentage
Upto 8 hrs.	570	57.00
8-10 hrs.	250	25.00
10-12 hrs.	180	18.00
Total	**1000**	**100.00**

Table 6.2 shows that 57 percentage of the total respondents work up to 8 hours;25 percentage of the respondents work upto 8 to 10 hours; the remaining 18 percentage of the women workers are working in the units upto 10 to 12 hours.

The table concludes that one half of the respondents work up to 8 hours, one-fourth of the respondents work upto 8 to 10 hours and one-fifth of the women workers are working upto 10 to 12 hours.

MODE OF BASIS FACILITIES

Every business organization has to provide basic facilities adequately to their workers. They includedrinking water facilities, rest room facilities and toilet facilities. The basic facilities of women workers are shown in the following table.

Table 6.3

Provision of Basic Facilities

Basic Facilities	No. of Respondents	Percentage
Drinking Water	1000	100
Rest Room	670	67
Toilet Facility	890	89

Table 6.3 shows the pattern of distribution of respondents on the basis of available basic facilities in the work spot. 100 percentage of the respondents are having drinking water facilities. 67 percentage of the respondents are having rest room facilities and 89 percentage of the respondents are satisfied withtoilet facilities.

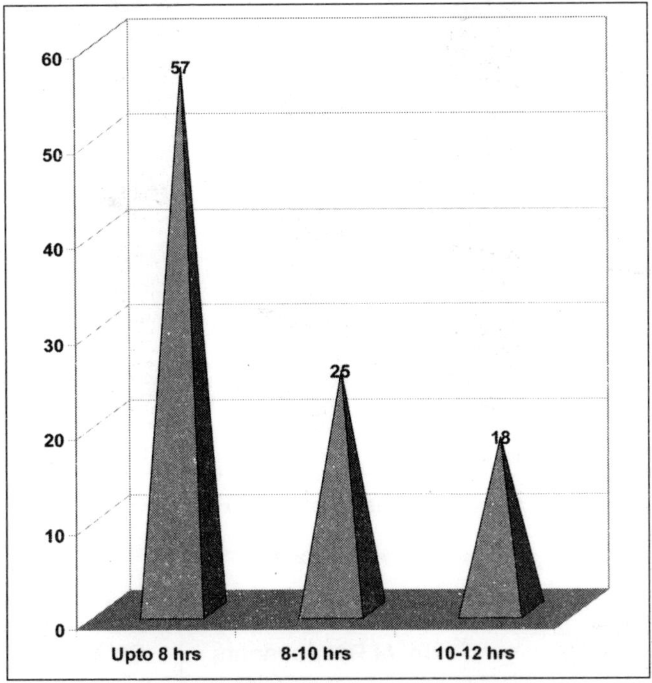

Fig. 6.1: Respondents and Time Spent

All the women workers haveenough drinking water facilities. Two-third of the respondents haverest room facilities and nine-tenth of the respondents have toilet facilities.

OUTLOOKOF WEEKLY LEAVE

Normally, all Sundays areholidays for the readymade garment workers. The following table reveals the respondents opinion about weakly leave.

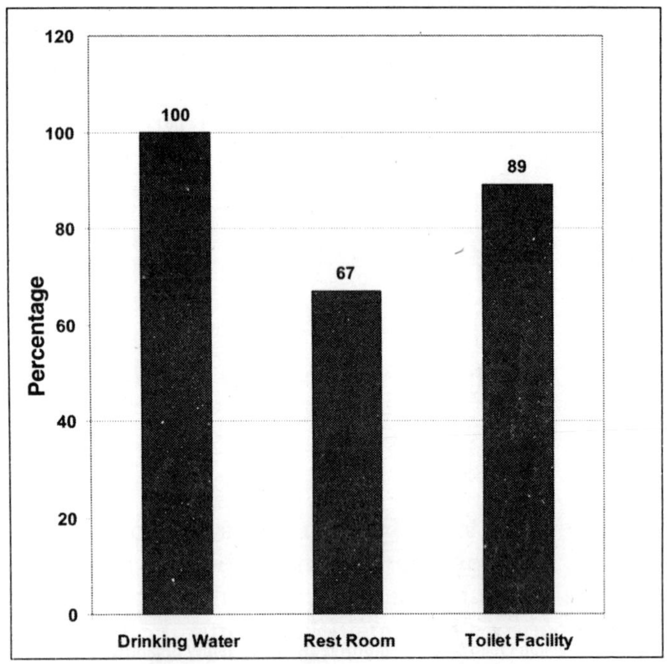

Fig. 6.2: Provision of Basic Facilities

Table 6.4

Respondents by Opinion of Weekly Leave

Opinion	No. of Respondents	Percentage
Yes	840	84
No	160	16
Total	**1000**	**100**

Table 6.4 reveals that the opinion about weekly leaves. Nearly 84 percentage of the respondents are getting weekly leave regularly whereas 16 percentage of the workers are not permitted weekly leave regularly.

Majority of the women workers are getting weekly leave and one-seventh of the women workers are not permitted weekly leave.

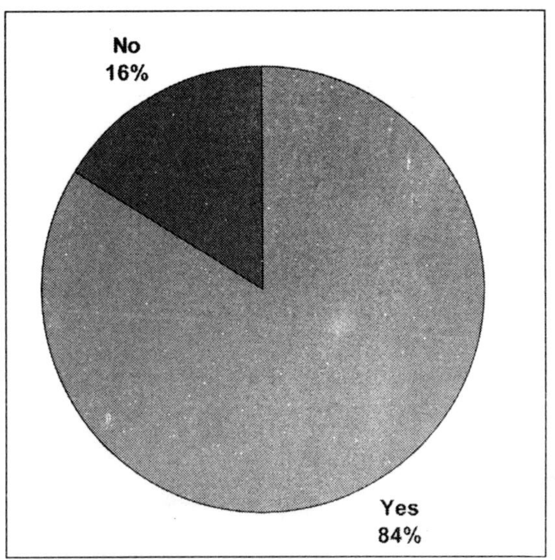

Fig. 6.3: Respondents by Opinion of Weekly Leave

RESPONDENTS OPINION ON NATIONAL HOLIDAYS

The respondents of readymade garmentworks enjoynational holidays like Pongal, Deepavali, Christmas, New Year, and Independence Day. It is given in the following table.

Table 6.5

National Holidays and Respondents Opinion

Opinion	No. of Respondents	Percentage
Yes	860	86
No	140	14
Total	**1000**	**100**

Table 6.5 reveals that the opinion about national holidays. 86 percentage of the respondents are getting national holidays and 14 percentage of the respondents are not permitted national holidays.

Majority of women workers of readymade garment are getting national holidays and one-seventh of the women workers are not getting national holidays.

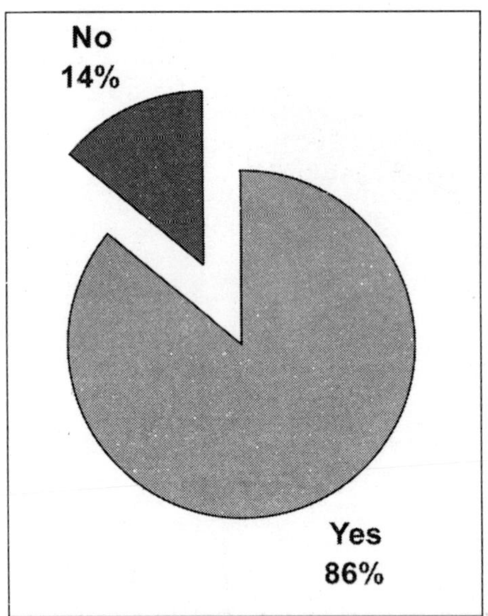

Fig. 6.4: National Holidays and Respondents Opinion

PERIODICITY OF WAGE PAYMENT

Wage means payment for services. Wage is the remuneration (or) reward of workers. The following table reveals the wage payment periodicity of women workers in readymade garment works.

Table 6.6

Periodicity of Wage Payment

Periodicity	No. of Respondents	Percentage
Daily	–	–
Weekly	730	73.00
Fortnightly	250	25.00
Monthly	20	2.00
Total	**1000**	**100.00**

The above table shows respondents' distribution on the basis of periodicity of wage payment. No one is receiving wage daily, 73 percentage of respondents are getting wage weekly, 25 percentage of respondents are getting wage fortnightly and two percentage of respondents are getting wage on monthly basis.

Most of the women workers are getting wage weekly, one-fourth of the women workers are getting wage fortnightly and a very few of them are getting wages on monthly basis.

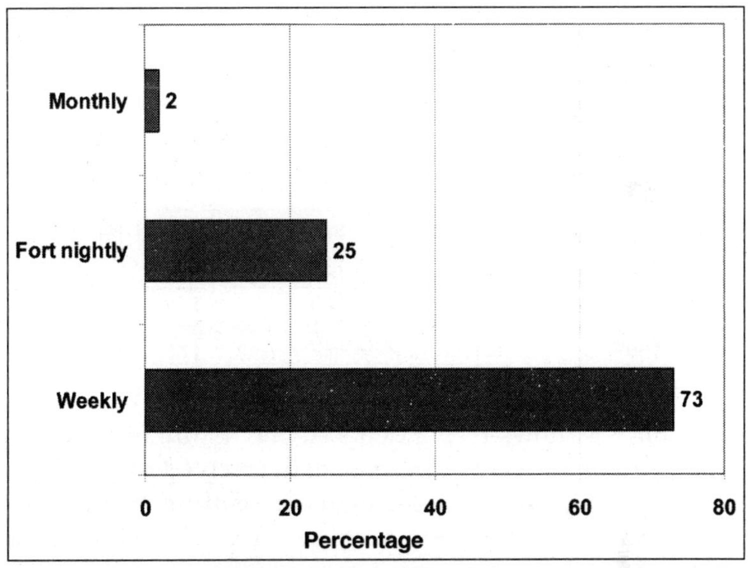

Fig. 6.5: Periodicity of Wage Payment

MONETARY BENEFIT

Monetary benefitssuch as bonus, incentive wages, medical expenses and loan and advances are additional benefits other than wages. The following table reveals monetary benefits other than wages of women worker in readymade garment works.

Table 6.7

Monetary Benifit

Opinion	No. of Respondents	Percentage
Yes	930	93.00
No	70	7.00
Total	1000	100.00

Table 6.7 shows the respondents' distribution on the basis of receiving monetary benefit other than wages; 93 percentage of the women workers are in receipt of monetary benefits.

Majority of the women workers of garmentworks are receiving monetary benefit other than wages and only a few of them are not granted any monetary benefits.

NATURE OF MONETARY BENEFIT

The monetary benefitsbeing paid to women workers are bonus, medical expense, OT wage, loan facilities and group insurance. This is presented in the following table.

Table 6.8

Nature of Monetary Benefit

Nature of Benefit	No. of Respondents	Percentage
Bonus	890/930	95.70
Medical Expenses	510/930	54.84
OT Wage	500/930	53.76
Loan Facility	440/ 930	47.31

Table 6.8 shows respondents by the nature of monetary benefit. Out of the 930 monetary benefit received respondents, 95.70 percentage of the respondents are getting bonus, 54.84 percentage of the women workers are getting medical expenses, 53.76 percentage of respondents are getting OT wage and the remaining 47.31 percentage of respondents are getting loan facilities.

The inference form the above table, majority of the respondents are in receipt of bonus, one half of the respondents are getting medical expenses, another one half of the respondents are getting OT wage and the remaining one half of the respondents are getting loan facilities.

FREE FOOD

Free food from canteen is being recognized all over the world as an essential part of industrial establishment. It provides great benefits from the point of view of health, efficiency, and well being of the workers. Besides, a canteen provides a meeting place for the workers of all department of a factory where they not only sit and take their meals, but also talk, rest and refresh their energies. As per the survey data a few of them are benefited through the free food scheme. The following table shows the data.

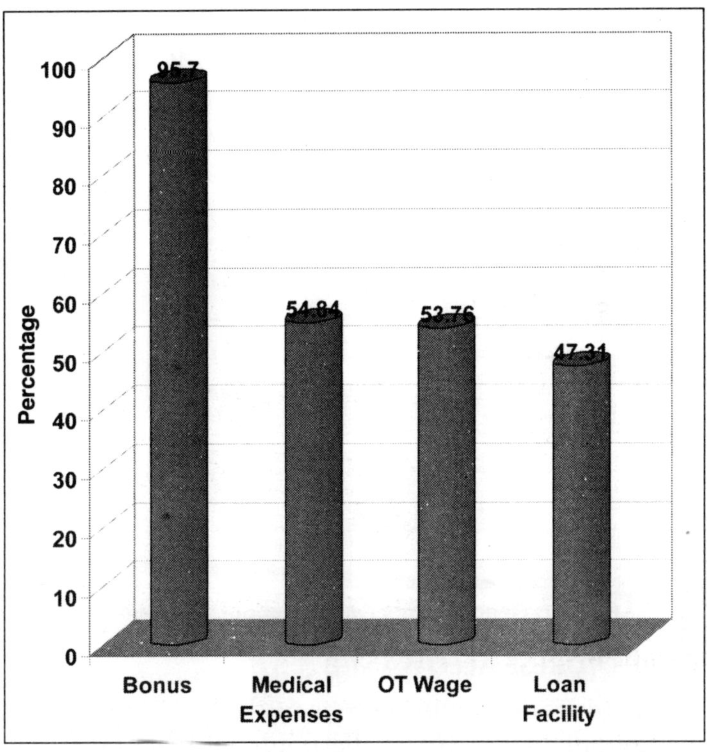

Fig. 6.6: Number of Respondents and Monetary Benefits

Table 6.9

Respondents Opinion about Free Food

Free Food	No. of Respondents	Percentage
Yes	160	16.00
No	840	84.00
Total	1000	100.00

Table 6.9 shows the respondents opinion about free food. 16 percentage of the women workers are getting free food and the remaining 84 percentage of the women workers are not getting free food.

Majority of the women workers of readymade garmentworks are not getting free food. Only one-seventh of the respondents are getting free food.

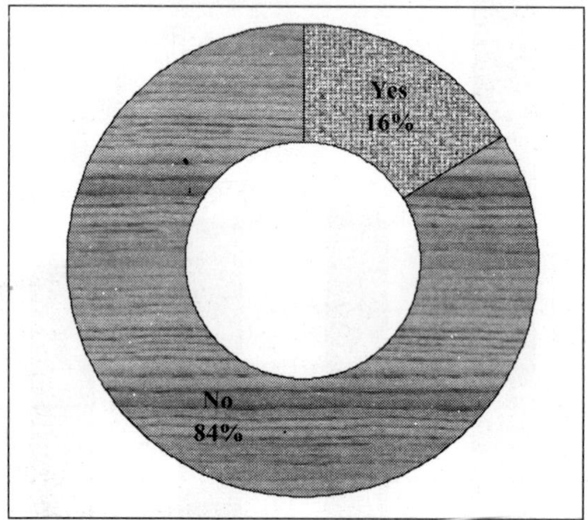

Fig. 6.7: Respondents Opinion about Free Food

FREE DRESS/DRESS ALLOWANCE

Free dress/dress allowance is not only a basic need, but also a fundamental right of the poor. But the high prices have kept it away for many, particularly the weaker sections of the society. Since the provision of dress/dress allowance to the people raises the quality of life and efficiency, the government has emphasized on the industrial establishments to provide dress/dress allowance facilities to its workers. Table 6.10 explains the free dress/dress allowance to the respondents.

Table 6.10

Respondents Opinion about Free Dress/Dress Allowance

Free Dress/Dress Allowance	No. of Respondents	Percentage
Yes	16	16
No	84	84
Total	**100**	**100**

The above table shows that out of the total 1000 sampled respondents, 16 percentage of the women workers are getting free dress and 84 percentage of the women workers are not getting free dress/dress allowance.

Majority of the women workers of readymade garmentworks are not getting free dress/dress allowance. One seventh of the respondents got free dress.

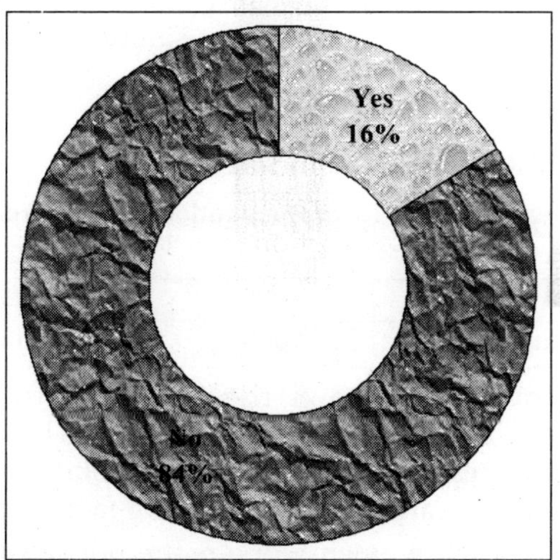

Fig. 6.8: Respondents Opinion about Free Dress/Dress Allowance

RESPONDENTS OPINION ABOUT THEIR ASSOCIATION

Readymade garment workers' association is fully functionalin Thoothukudi. But many of the respondents are not tied asthe members of this association. The following table explains the opinion about the association membership.

Table 6.11

Respondents Opinion about the Association Membership

Association Member	No. of Respondents	Percentage
Yes	50	5.00
No	950	95.00
Total	**1000**	**100.00**

Table 6.11 shows the respondents on the basis of association membership. Only five percentage of respondents are the members of the association and 95 percentage of respondents are not the association members.

Majority of women workers of readymade garmentworks are not the members of association.

SAFETY MEASURES

Safety means "protecting employees from injuries caused by work related accidents". Majority of women workers of readymade works do not have any safety measures. It is shown in the following Table.

Table 6.12

Respondents and Safety Measures

Safety Measures	No. of Respondents	Percentage
Yes	20	2.00
No	980	98.00
Total	**1000**	**100.00**

The above table shows the respondents by safety measures. Only two percentage of respondents have satisfied by safety measures. Majority (98%) of respondents have not satisfied about the safety measures in the factory premises.

Majority of the women workers are not satisfied about the safety measures existing in the factory premises.

OPINION ABOUT SATISFACTION OF THEIR PAY

Satisfaction refers to 'Fullness of mind'. In the study area most of the respondents are not satisfied by their pay. Table 6.13 explains the respondents' opinion about the monthly pay.

Table 6.13

Opinion about the Satisfaction of their Pay

Opinion	No. of Respondents	Percentage
Yes	400	40.00
No	600	60.00
Total	**1000**	**100.00**

Table 6.13 shows the respondent satisfaction about their pay. Out of the total, 40 percentage of the women workers are satisfied by their pay and 60 percentage of the women workers have not satisfied by their pay.

Majority of the women workers of readymade garment work are not satisfied by their pay. Two-fifth of the respondents are satisfied by their monthly salary.

EDUCATIONAL STATUS AND JOB SATISFICATION

H_0: There is no significant difference between educational status and job satisfaction of women workers of readymade garment works.

Test: Chi – Square Test

Table 6.14

Relationship between Educational Status and Job Satisfaction

Education	Job Satisfaction		
	Yes	No	Total
Illiterate	24	40	64
Elementary	298	50	348
Higher Elementary	227	110	337
Secondary	83	40	123
Higher secondary	91	25	116
College	7	5	12
Total	**730**	**270**	**1000**

The calculated chi-square value 79.494 is greater than table value (11.01) at 5% level of significant. Therefore, the Null hypothesis is rejected.

Consequently, there is significant association between education status and job satisfaction. Therefore the third hypothesis that 'There is no significant difference between educational status and job satisfaction of women workers of readymade garment works' is disproved.

MONTHLY INCOME AND JOB SATISFACTION

H_0: There is no significant difference between monthly income of women workers and job satisfaction.

Test: Chi – Square Test

Table 6.15

Relationship between Monthly Income and Job Satisfaction

Monthly Income	Job Satisfaction		
	Yes	No	Total
Below 3,000	101	34	135
3,000-6,000	420	95	515
6,000-9,000	125	110	235
Above 9,000	84	31	115
Total	**730**	**270**	**1000**

The calculated value 66.124 is greater than the critical value 7.815 at 5% level of significant. Hence it is found that the null hypothesis is rejected, that, there is significant association between monthly income of women workers and job satisfaction of readymade garment works. Therefore, the fourth hypothesis reading 'There is no significant difference between monthly income of women workers and job satisfaction' becomes invalid.

MARITAL STATUS AND JOB SATISFACTION

Ho: There is no significant difference between marital status and job satisfaction of women workers of readymade garment works.

Test: Chi-Square Test

Table 6.16

Relationship between Marital Status and Job Satisfaction

Marital Status	Job Satisfaction		
	Yes	No	Total
Married	390	153	543
Un Married	340	117	457
Total	730	270	1000

The calculated value 0.736 is less than table value 3.841 at 5% level of significant. Hence it is found that the null hypothesis is accepted, that there is no significant association between marital status and job satisfaction. Therefore, the fifth hypothesis that 'There is no significant difference between marital status and job satisfaction of women workers of readymade garment works' is proved.

SUGGESTIONS FOR BETTERMENT

The following table shows the readymade garment women workers'suggestions for improving the standard of living and their work.

Table 6.17

Suggestions for Betterment

Suggestions	No of Respondents	Percentage to Total
Govt. Fixing Minimum Wages	365	36.50
Labour Union	225	22.50
Loan Facilities	150	15.00
Alternative Job	160	26.00
Total	1000	100.00

As found in the table, 36.50 percentage of readymade garment women workers want the Government to fix the minimum wages. Efficient labour union is expected to improve the standard of living according to 22.50 percentage of readymade garment women workers. 15 percentage of readymade garment women workers feel that loan facilities with low rate of interest are the next suggestion. The remaining 26 percentage of readymade garment women workers want alternative job because the tailoring work is experienced as a painful work.

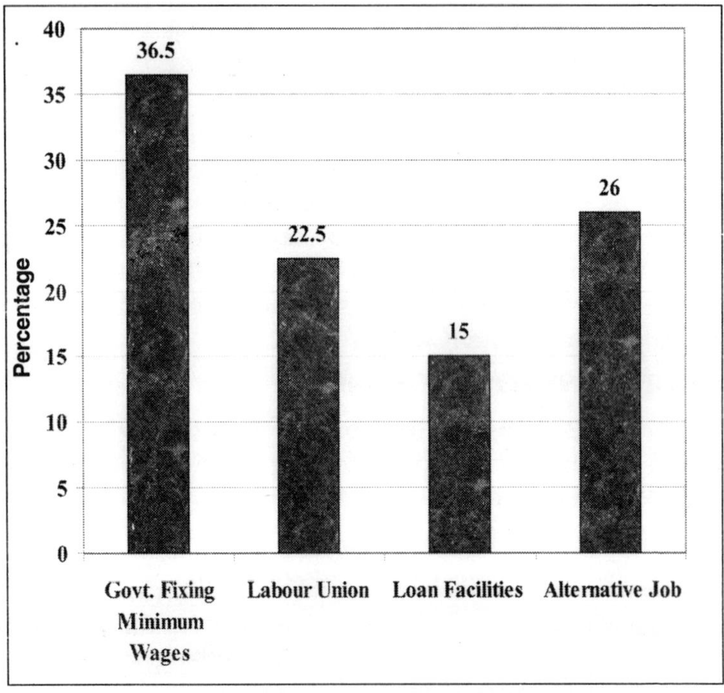

Fig. 6.9: Suggestions for Betterment

The respondents are of the feeling that efficient labour union should involve to improve their standard of living. One-seventh of the workers also feel that loan facilities with low rate of interest may be allowed for their betterment.

Occupational Hazards in Readymade Garment Works

OCCUPATIONAL HAZARDS

Occupational disease is a disease common among workers engaged in a particular occupation. They are caused by the conditions of that occupation. They are rather slow and generally cumulative in their effects. Occasionally some occupational diseases become more critical and serious enough to cause even death.

Because of their continuous work, the workers often complain of 'back pain' as the commonest one. Another major ailment for the tailoring workers is eye problem. They also complain of skin diseases, urinal infection and respiratory diseases. The status of having occupational diseases of women workers is classified in the following table.

Table 7.1

Occupational Hazards

Opinion	No. of Respondents	Percentage
Yes	730	73.00
No	270	27.00
Total	**1000**	**100.00**

From the above table it is observed that 73 percentage of readymade garments women workers have occupational diseases of one form or other and only 27 percentage of them are reported to have no occupational disease in the present job. Hence, majority of the readymade garments women workers are suffering occupational diseases in the present job.

TYPE OF HEALTH PROBLEM

The readymade garments women workers are engaged in tailoring industry due to unavailability of other alternative employment opportunities. They are trapped in the vicious cycle of debts and suffer from occupational health hazards. Majority of the readymade garments women workers are suffering more than one occupational diseases with the present job.

The problems from the point of view of the readymade garments women workers engaged in tailoring work in the study area are listed giving weightage points to various problems as follows:

1 – Rank = 5 points
2 – Rank = 4 points
3 – Rank = 3 points
4 – Rank = 2 points
5 – Rank = 1 point

Table 7.2

Health Problems Faced by women readymade garment workers

Problem	I	II	III	IV	V	Total
Back Pain	400	160	220	100	120	1000
Skin Disease	120	220	180	240	240	1000
Eye Problem	120	200	240	220	220	1000
Urinal Infection	160	160	160	240	280	1000
Respiratory Diseas	200	260	200	200	140	1000
Total	**1000**	**1000**	**1000**	**1000**	**1000**	**1000**

On the basis of the points given and ranks obtained, the total rank of each problem was calculated. The total rank status was thus derived by the total number of respondents for each problem. Among the five factors given in the schedule, the one which had the highest mean score was identified as the major problem faced by the readymade garments women workers.

CALCULATION OF GARRETT MEAN SCORE

For the present study, the Garrett Ranking Technique[1] was employed to findout the influencing factor. The Garrett Ranking Technique was also adopted to identify the most common factor. The formula for calculating Garrett Ranking is:

$$\text{Present Position} = \frac{100\,(Rij - 0.5)}{Nj}$$

where,

Rij – Rank given for the ith reason by jth respondents

Nj – Number of factors ranked by jth respondents

Following Table shows that Garrett mean score of each problem:

Table 7.3

Garrett Mean Score and Problems Faced by Readymade Garment Women Workers

Problems	Garrett Ranking Mean Score	Rank
Back Pain	27.31	I
Skin Diseases	20.07	IV
Eye Problem	22.22	II
Urinal Infection	19.78	V
Respiratory Disease	20.62	III

It is inferred from the above table; among the various problems met by the readymade garments women workers, back pain is the main problem. The second one determined is eye sickness. Respiratory disease is another problem that has also been faced by a portion of the readymade garment women workers. Skin disease and urinal infection are considered as the least problems faced by the women workers. The following figure depicts the Garrett Mean Score.

A majority of the tailors are affected by back pain. One-third of the respondents have eye problem, one-tenth of the respondents have respiratory disease and few of them are suffering from skin diseases and urinal infection.

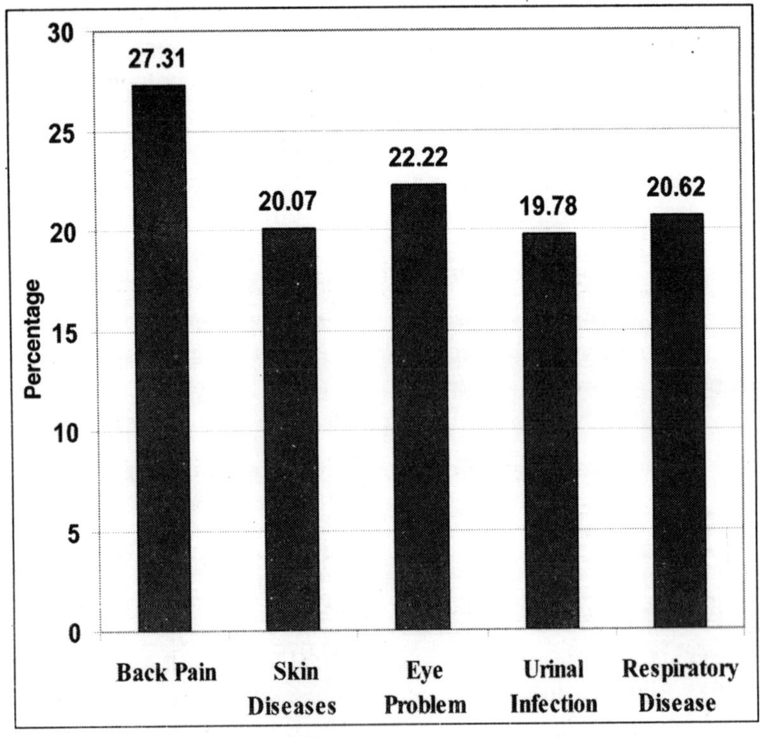

Fig. 7.1: Garrett Mean Score - Problems Faced by readymade garments women workers

RELATIONSHIP BETWEEN AGE AND HEALTH PROBLEM

H_0: There is no significant difference between age and health problem of the women workers in readymade garment industries.

Test: Chi-Square Test

Table 7.4

Relationship between Age and Health Problem

Age	Health Problem		
	Yes	No	Total
Up to 15	16	20	36
15-25	249	95	354
25-35	281	80	361
35-45	173	50	223
45-55	5	20	15
55-65	6	5	11
Total	**730**	**270**	**1000**

$$\chi^2 = \frac{\Sigma(O - E)^2}{E}$$

O = Observed frequency

E = Expected Frequency

$$EF = \frac{\text{Row total} \times \text{Column total}}{\text{Grand Total}}$$

The calculated chi-square value (11.1) is greater than the table value (9.488) at 5% level of significant. Therefore, the hypothesis is rejected. Hence, there is significant association between age and health problem of the women workers. For that reason the second hypothesis becomes invalid.

The profession of the women workers in readymade garment industry is strenuous and difficult. Though they have other problems like poor job security, poor basic facilities, leave problems, wage problems, work related ailments are also common. During the survey, the respondents demanded that government should give liberal ration at subsidized rate, housing facilities, free insurance coverage, medical allowance, subsidy loans, educational facilities for their children and some other welfare measures for the employees.

Electronic sewing machines were introduced in the late eighties together with the training of women workers in Readymade Garment works in handling of modern machine. In late eighties an important technological development took place, namely button holding, button sewing and zip fixing. These technics should be extended for other fields of the garment works.

REFERENCES

1. Garrett E. Henry, Statistics in Psychology and Education, Vakils Feffer and Simons Private Limited, Bombay, 1969, pp. 328-331.

8

Conclusion

With the acceptance of women and their participation in work force as a necessity, there is application of their tremendous skills potentials. The participation of women in the work in the study area was intended not merely to improve their quality of life but to empower indecision making in their family. From the analysis of the empirical data, the women participation is found to be satisfactory. Higher level of internal consistency among women employment was observed in work contribution and quality of work life in the case of public sector. Thus it may be concluded that women workers in public sector appeared much more satisfied in work force participation compared to private sector women employees.

In both public and private sector, women employees are in a positive frame of mind to take independent decisions which in turn ensure their empowerment in decision making in their family.

FINDINGS

Socio-demogrphic Characteristics of Workers

The study shows that, about one-third of the workers are under the age group of 25-35 years and another one-third of the respondents are under the age group of 15-25 years. One-fourth of the respondents are under the age group of 35-45 years.

Majority of the respondents belong to backward community. One-seventh of the respondents belong to most backward community and one-fourth of the respondents are from the schedule community.

The study further found out that four-fifth of the respondents are Hindus, one-fifth of the respondents are Christians and a meager percentage of the respondents are Islam by religion.

About their marital status, it is understood that, about one-half of the respondents are married and the other one-half of the respondents are unmarried.

Majority of the women readymade garments workers have studied up to primary level. About one-third of the respondents have studied up to middle level education and about one-seventh of the respondents have studied up to secondary level education. One-fifteenth of the women workers are illiterates and a few of them have studied up to degree level.

One-fifth of the respondents families have upto 3 members i.e; small sized family, two-third has 4-6 members i.e., medium sized family and one-seventh have above 6 members i.e., large sized family.

Majority of the respondents are in the service for five years, one-fourth of the respondents are in the service between 5-10 years, one-fifth of the respondents are in the service between 10-15 years and one-seventh of them are in the service above 15 years.

Majority of the readymade women workers are doing stitching work. One-tenth of the workers are doing cloth cutting and another one-tenth women workers are doing button holing and few of them are doing other works like embroidery, button sewing and zip fixing.

INCOME AND SAVINGS PATTERN OF THE WOMEN WORKERS

Majority of the readymade women workers have time rate and one-fifth of the workers have piece rate.

The study inferred that one-half of the respondents earn Rs.3,000 to 6,000 per month, one-fourth of the respondents earning between Rs. 6,000 to 9,000, one-seventh of the respondents earn below Rs. 3,000 per month and one-tenth of the respondents earn above Rs. 9,000 per month.

The Gini concentration is 0.2324. This reveal that the degree of inequality is low ie, 0.23. On the whole, the data suggests that the income distribution among the four groups of households show a low variation.

The χ^2 test employed affirms that there is a significant difference in the level of age and income. Therefore the first hypothesis namely 'There is no significant difference between the level of age and income' is disproved.

The study concluded that about one-fourth of them are earning below Rs.25,000, about one-third of them are earning between Rs. 25,000 to 50,000, about one-seventh of them are earning between Rs. 50,000 to 75,000, about one-fifths of them are earning between Rs. 75,000 to 1,00,000 and one-tenth of them earn above 1,00,000 per year.

Majority of the total income is spent on food items. One-tenth of the total income is spent on clothes another one-tenth of the total income is spent on religious and social functions. One-twentieth of the total income is spent on fuel and lighting, another one-twentieth of the total income is spent on education and a little portion of the total income is spent on medicine, entertainment and others.

It has been found that the multiple regression is significant in terms of its 'F' value which is calculated to be 29.524 with an R^2 value of 0.582 explaining nearly 58 per cent of the variations in the family expenditure of women workers. All the co-efficients are found significant at 5 percent level except the constant term. According to the estimated model, the total expenditure increases by Rs. 12.68 for every one unit of the increase in the family size. For one rupee of increase in the family income the total expenditure increases by 72 paise. Every one-rupee increase in the amount of borrowing increases the family's expenditure by nearly 29 paise.

Majority of the women workers save up to Rs. 3,000 per year and one-third of the respondents save Rs. 5,000 to 10,000 per annum, one-seventh of the respondents save Rs.10,000 to 15,000 and one-tenth of the respondents save above Rs. 15,000 per annum. One-tenth of the women workers have no savings at all.

A majority of the respondents save their money in chit funds. One-third of the respondents save their money in chit funds. One-tenth of the respondents save their money in post office. One-fifth of the respondents save their money in bank and one-fourth of the workers save their money in LIC. One-tenth of the respondents have no saving at all.

Most of the loan amounts are availed by the readymade garments women workers in the study area only from self help groups. One-fifths of the loan amounts are taken from co-operative bank. Another one-fifths of the loan amount received from self help group and one-tenth of the loan amount received from friends and relatives.

EXPLOITATION OF WOMEN WORKERS

Majority of the respondents expressed the need of the job after knowing the backwardness of the family. One-fourth of the respondents expressed that they got this job for easy work. One-fifth of the respondents expressed that they preferred this job for better wages. One-seventh of the respondents expressed that they accepted this job for the reason that they were forced by husband and family.

A majority of the respondents are selected to the job for having completed their Diploma courses in tailoring or dress making. One-third of the respondents are selected on the ground of proper training. One-fourth of the respondents are selected for their previous experience. One-tenth of the respondents are selected for the reason that they belong to the same village.

A huge majority of the respondents expressed that they face problem with their employers. One-tenth of the respondents expressed that they face problem with employer in often. One-fourth of the respondents expressed that they have no problem with their employers.

Majority of the respondents have problems related to wages. One-fifth of the respondents have problems related to leave. One-tenth of the workers opinion that employer is not satisfied with their work. A very few of them opined that employer is not satisfied with their behaviour.

Majority of the readymade garments women workers make have occupational diseases and a few of them have no occupational disease in the tailoring industry.

Majority of the tailors are affected by back pain. One-third of the respondents have eye problem, one-tenth of the respondents have respiratory disease and few of them suffering from skin diseases and urinal infection.

The relationship between age health problems analysed through chi-square test. The calculated chi-square value (11.1) is greater than the table value (9.488) at 5% level of significant. Therefore the hypothesis is rejected. Hence, there is significant association between age and health problem of the women workers. Therefore the second hypothesis namely 'There is no significant difference between age and health problem of the women workers in readymade garments' is unvalued.

Majority of the readymade garments women workers expressed that they are not affected by the sexual harassment. One-third of the readymade garments women workers expressed that they are affected by the sexual harassment with employer and other men co-workers.

Majority of women workers of readymade garment works do not have job satisfaction and one-fourth of the respondents are satisfied the readymade garment works.

Majority of the women workers prefer to say that "As long as the readymade works continue they would work". One-fourth of the respondents are opined "as long as they like to work they would continue" and one portion of the respondents say "they may be expelled at any time".

The study concluded that one half of the respondents work up to 8 hours, one-fourth of the respondents are work upto 8 to 10 hours and one-fifth of the women workers are working in the units upto 10 to 12 hours.

All the women workers have drinking water facilities. Two-third of the respondents have rest room facilities and nine-tenth of the respondents have toilet facilities.

Majority of the women workers are getting weekly leave and one-seventh of the women workers are not getting any weekly leave.

Majority of women workers of readymade garment are getting national holidays and one-seventh of the women workers are not getting national holidays.

Most of the women workers are getting wage weekly, one-fourth of the women workers are getting wage fortnightly and a very few of them are getting wages monthly basis.

Majority of the women workers of readymade garment works are getting monetary benefit other than wages. Few of them are not getting any monetary benefits.

Majority of the respondents are getting bonus, one half of the respondents are getting medical expenses, another one half of the respondents are getting OT wage and another one half of the respondents are getting loan facilities.

Majority of the women workers of readymade garment works are not getting free food. One-seventh of the respondents are getting free food.

Majority of the women workers of readymade garment works are not getting free dress/dress allowance. One seventh of the respondents got free dress.

Majority of women workers of readymade garment works are not member of association. Few of them are the member of the association.

Majority of the women workers are not satisfied about the safety measures in the factory premises. Few of them satisfied about the safety measures.

Majority of the women workers of readymade garment work are not satisfied by their pay. Two-fifth of the respondents has satisfied by their monthly salary.

The relationship between educational status and job satisfaction, chi-square test is employed. The results concluded that there is significant association between education status and job satisfaction. Therefore the third hypothesis that 'There is no significant difference between educational status and job satisfaction of women workers of readymade garment works' is disproved.

The relationship between monthly income and job satisfaction, chi-square test is employed. Hence it is found that the null hypothesis is rejected, that, there is significant association between monthly income of women workers and job satisfaction of readymade garment works. Therefore, the fourth hypothesis namely 'There is no significant difference between monthly income of women workers and job satisfaction' is invalid.

The relationship between marital status and job satisfaction another chi-square test is employed. It is found that the null hypothesis is accepted, that there is no significant association between marital status and job satisfaction. Therefore, the fifth hypothesis that 'There is no significant difference between marital status and job satisfaction of women workers of readymade garment works' is proved.

Majority of the readymade garment women workers want the Government to fix the minimum wages. One-fourth of the respondents are wanting alternative job because the tailoring work is painful work. Another one-fourth of the respondents are feeling that efficient labour union is expected to improve the standard of living. One-seventh of the readymade garment women workers feel that loan facilities with low rate of interest are the next suggestion.

SUGGESTIONS

On the basis of the findings few tentative suggestion are offered which may help to enhance/ensure the participation of women workforce in such industries.

- The government must insist the employers to provide better and more secure working and living conditions to the workers.

- Legislation regarding the compulsory group insurance, family pension and paid holidays must be introduced.
- The employers should be statutorily asked to make provision for medical facilities. Such medical facilities should be made available to the readymade garment women workers at a nearby place.
- The Government should fix and enforce the minimum rates of wages to the readymade garment women workers. The Act should be more effectively implemented. The prevailing minimum wage rate should be immediately revised to cope up with the rising prices. The act should ensure equal pay for 'equal work' and thus avoid discrimination in payment of wages on the basis of sex.
- In order to reduce the unemployment, various schemes with regard to rural development such as Sampoorna Grameen Rozgar Yojana (SGRY), Swarnajayanti Gram Swarozgar Yojana (SGSY), TRYSEM, DWACRA etc should be introduced.

All efforts to promote participation initiatives can be viewed only in the context of economic independence and empowerment of women. Women in India are not able to contribute their best to the development of the society. It is because they are mostly back ward in education, and in social, economic and political spheres. Further, it is observed that the high incidence of illiteracy among women constituted as one of the greatest barriers to their development. It limited their scope for work force participation. As such government should take more efforts to promote women participation in work force. Women may be given equal opportunities for education, training, extension and decisions making. Government can enact laws which ensure equal rights & opportunities for women with men in all jobs opportunities.

It is suggested the government should promote exclusive organization and programmers for women's participation. Government can support quasi- government pseudo-government (co-operations), non-governmental and self-help groups for women. Further it is suggested the Governments grants and aids may also be routed through exclusive women's organizations where ever they are prevailing.

The present study, for the many reasons outlined above, could be claimed to be opportune. India is a country with a heart. Mystery ancient culture placed women on a pedestal and glorified motherhood. But, the modern realities are quite different. Women have been at the receiving end Male chauvinism and gender bias had often gone against the aspiration of women to play their roles in society. It is in this context that a study that looks at the various options of women's empowerment that lead to their ultimate liberation, strikes the right note the best is yet to be.

CONCLUSION

The readymade garment women workers are prepared to work in readymade industry in spite of poor wage rates and other bitter conditions. Moreover, the readymade garment industries are unable to provide works throughout the year. In the absence of work, the workers have to seek some other jobs and they are forced to migrate to some other places in Thoothukudi district in search of other opportunities in industries. With all the evidences summarized so far, it is concluded that the conditions of readymade garment women workers have to be improved. It is to be noted that the above suggestions, if implemented effectively will yield the desired results and solve the problems of readymade garment women workers.

Bibliography

BOOKS

Ahmed, Rural Employment – Non Farm Sector p.np: 421 Deep & Deep Publication Pvt. Ltd. New Delhi, 1985.

Alakh N. Sharma and Seema Singh: "Women and Work Changing Scenario in India", B.R. Publishing Corporations, New Delhi, 1993, P. 159.

Ganiger S.B: Research Investigator and Rajeswari N.V. Research Officer, "Female Employment in Non-agricultural Sector in Urban Karnataka", Population Research Centre, JSS Institute of Economic Research Vidyagir, Bharwed – 4, Karnataka, 1996.

John W.Mellor." The New Economics of Growth; A Strategy for India and the Developing World", Cornell University Press, Ithaca, New York 1976, p. 73.

Lalitha. N., "Rural Non-Farm Sector in India-Gandhigram Experiment" (Ed) Venkata Ravi. R, Sivaram.P. Sunderraj. D., Empowering Kanishka Publishers, Distributors, New Delhi (2006) pp. 219-233.

Krishna Murthy, J., "Women in Colonial India", Calcutta: Oxford University Press, 1999, p. 6.

Mary Billington, F., "Women in India", Air Marks Book Agency, New Delhi, 1991, p. 9-11.

Mittal A.C., " Rural Economy" Vista International Publishing House Delhi, 2006, p. 104.

Meenakshisundaram N.: "Working Conditions of Women in Tanneries", in Sudhir M.A. and Balakrishnan A.: (eds) Empowerment of Rural Female Labour Force, Anmol Publications, New Delhi, 2002, pp. 64-67.

Malvika Karlaker, "Poverty and Women's Workers –A Study of Sweeper Women in Delhi", Vikas Publication, New Delhi Vol. II, 1982, pp. 112-120.

Nancy David, Unorganized Women Workers: Problems and Prospects", (Ed) Tripathy, S.N., Unorganized Women Labour in India, Discovery Publishing House, New Delhi, 1996, pp. 15-26.

Saraswathy N: Women Labour in Unorganized Sector Needs Reappraisal of Labour Laws" in Sudhir M.A. and Balakrishnan A.: (eds) Empowerment of Rural Female Labour Force, Anmol Publications, New Delhi, 2002, pp. 104-104.

Satyendra P.Gupta. Possibilities of Rural Development Through on Farm and Non-farm Employment. An Economic Evaluation (Rural Employment – The Non-farm Sector by M, Koteswara Rao) Deepand Deep Publications Private Ltd., New Delhi 2000 pp. 73-83.

Srinivasa Rao. K "Rural Non-farm Employment and Residual Sector Hypothesis A Study Rural Employment. The Non-farm Sector, Edited by M. Koteswara Rao, Deep and Deep Publishers Private Ltd,. Delhi, pp. 161-178.

Srinivase Rao.K. "Determinants of Rural Non-form Employment in India – Regression Analysis" Rural Employment; The Non-Farm sector Edited By Kotesware Rao .M., Deep and Deep publications Private Ltd., New Delhi 2000, pp. 138-153.

Samal C.Kishore." Features and Determinants of Rural Non-farm Sector in India and Orissa. A Survey" Deep and Deep Publications Private Ltd., New Delhi 2000, pp. 84-133.

Tripathy.S.N., "Women Labour in Construction Sector: A Study in Orissa", (Ed) Tripathy.S.N., Unorganized Women Labour in India, Discovery Publishing House, New Delhi, 1996, pp. 105-122.

Tripathy S.N : and Patnaik, P.K., "Socio-Economic Profile of Fisher Women Community of Krushna Prasad Block (Orissa) in Unorganized Women Labour in India, Discovery Publishing House, New Delhi, 1996, pp. 123-140.

JOURNALS

Atmanad: "Women Labour Force – Trend and Pattern of Employment", Khadi Gramodyog the Journal of Rural Economy, Vol. 35, No. 6, March 1990, p. 247.

Asfak Hussian, "Exploitation of Women and Child Labour in Beedi Industry in Samserganj", Social Welfare, 34: January 1987, p. 9.

Arul Kamaraj, J.M., and Muralitharan, "Unorganised Women in Match Industry of Virudhunagar", Social Welfare, Vol. 52, No. 2, May 2005, pp. 13-16.

Baij Nath Singh: "Under Valuation of Work and Status of Rural Women: A Study", Southern Economist, Vol. 44, March 1, 2006, p. 23.

Chaitalipal, "Informal Sector and the Women Experiences of Delhi Construction Workers", Women's Link, Vol. 6, No. 4, 2000, pp. 2-8.

Dharmalingam. A, "Female Beedi Workers in a South Indian Village", Economic and Political Weekly, Vol. XXVIII, No. 27 & 28, 1993, pp. 1461-1468.

Darshan Singh: "Strategies for Empowering Women Workers", "Social Welfare" Vol. 52, No. 2, May 2005, p. 8.

Debal K. Singharoy and Prava Agarwal, "Self Employment for Rural Women", Yojana, Volume 33, No. 9, May 1969.

Director: Labour Bureau, "Study on the Working and Living Conditions of Workers in Bakery Industry in India", Controller of Publication, Civil Lines, Delhi, 1995.

Edward Nission, An Assessment of Economic Development. The Non-agricultural Sector Vs: The Agriculture Sector. The Indian Economic Journal Vol. 41 (4), 1997.

Harbans Singh, "The Impact of Rural Labourers and Socio-economic Conditions", Journal of Asian Studies, August, 1999, pp. 110-126.

Janette Moritz: "Women Workers in the Waste Economy", Economic and Political Weekly, Vol. 17, No. 1, April-June 1995, pp.19-31.

Jayam Kannan & Ilango. P., (1990) "Health Hazards of Women Working in Beedi Industries", Social Welfare, Vol. 36, No. 12, pp. 10-11.

Jeyaraman R., Ajay Sethy, V., "Role of Self-help Groups in Fisher Women Development", Peninsular Economists Tamilnadu Veterinary and Animal University, Tuticorin, Vol. 12, No. 2, 2005, pp. 196-200.

Jatindra Nath Saikia, "Handloom and Textile Sector of Assam: An Analysis", Southern Economist, Vol. 46, No. 14, 2010, pp. 41-44.

Jeet Sing Mann, "Welfare and Protective Measures Pertaining to the Construction Workers in India" National Law University, Jodhpur Raj, 2000, pp. 1-5.

Jeyaraj T.R. and Malathi.N, "Female Labour Problems and Prospective in Unorganized Sector of Cuddalore District, Tamil Nadu", Peninsular Economist,Vol. 12, No. 2, 1997, pp. 160-167.

Kamal Vattta and R.S.Sidhu "Rural Non-Farm Employment, Income Distribution and Poverty: Micro Level Evidence from Punjab" Indian Journal of Agricultural Economics, Vol. 65, No. 4, October-December 2010, pp. 694-709.

Kaptan S.S.: A Case Study of Amaravathi City: The Income: Wages and Working Conditions of Women Workers in the Unorganized Sector", Social Welfare, May 1990, pp. 29-31.

Kusugal.N.S and Birader R.R., "Rural Non-Farm Employment for Women in India: An Analysis of its Size and Determinants", Southern Economist, Vol. 49, No. 11, 2010, pp. 8-12.

Kumar.D., "Status of Women in India", Kisan World, Vol. 31, No. 1, 2004, p. 26.

Kamalakannan, K., "Women Construction Work in Tamilnadu" Social Welfare, Vol. 54, No. 2, May 2005, pp. 16-18.

Karunanithi G., "Child Labour in Melapalayam", Social Welfare, 35: 1990, pp. 10-11.

Karunanithi, "Child Labour in North Arcot Ambedkar District: An In-depth Study of Pledged Children in Beedi Works", (Project Report Submitted to Indian Council of Social Science Research, 1993), pp. 156-171.

Limbadri.R, "Socio-economic Profile of Beedi Workers: A Micro Study", Southern Economist, Vol. 46, No. 14, 2007, pp. 28-32.

Lalitha N., "Women in the Unorganized Manufacturing Sector in India – A Sectoral Analysis", The Indian Journal of Labour Economics, Vol. 32, No. 4, 1999, pp. 641-650.

Lawrence Mary, "Status of Working Women", Kissan World, Vol. 23, No. 12, Dec., p. 34.

Manipal, "Social Development of Rural Women in India", Kuruskhetra, Volume. 52, No. 9, July 2004.

Manimekalai N., and Sundari S. Female Labour Force in the Unorganized Sector of Mat Industries, Some Evidence", The Indian Journal of Social Work, Vol. II, No. 2, April 1991, pp. 195-202.

Manim Mekalai N.: and Sundari S.: "Female Labour Force in the Unorganized Sector of Mat Industry – Some Evidence", The Indian Journal of Social Work, Vol. LII, No. 2, April 1991, pp. 195-202.

Mohandas. M, and Praveenkumar P.V., "Impact of Co-operativisation on Working Conditions Study of Beedi Industry in Kerala", Economic and Political Weekly, Vol. 27, No. 26, 1992, pp. 1333-1337.

Moli. G.K.: "Labour Force in India", The Gender Gap, Samyukta, A Journal of Women's Studies, Vol. 4, No. 2, July 2004, pp. 53-56.

Mangaiyarkarasi, V., "Women Industrial Workers", Social Welfare, Vol. 50, No. 2, 2003, pp. 26, 27.

Narasimhalu K. and Sathya Murthy G. "Performance of Match Industry – A Case Study of Chitoor District", Khadi Gramodyog, September, 1991, pp. 484-490.

Nalini G.S., "Social Security for Unorganized Sector: A Micro Study", Southern Economist, Vol. 49, No. 17, 2011, pp. 14-16.

Nalinadavi and Jagathambal, "Health and Financial Problems Faced by Unorganized Women Workers" Research High Lights, Vol. 10, No. 2, April 2000, pp. 60-63.

Neerja, Chaudhury, "Beedi Makers in Madhya Pradesh", Hindustan Weekly, 31 August 1980, p. 3.

Nirmala Banerjee, "Trend in Women's Employment- Some Macro Level Observations", Economic and Political Weekly, 1989, April, p. 71-81.

Pitchaimuthu S., "Child Labour in Beedi Making Industries", Peninsular Economist (Tiruchirapalli, Association of Economists, 1987-88), p. 79.

Preeti Rustagi: "Women Employment in Unorganized Sector, Some Issues", Social Action, Vol. 47, April-June 1997, pp. 166-179.

Prasanna.N. & Jeyanthi. S., "Impact of Gender Prejudice on the Employment Status of Women in the Urban Unorganized Sector", Southern Economist, Vol. 49, 2010, pp. 36-38.

Prayag Mehta, "Mortgage Child Labour of Vellore Women Beedi Workers' Tale of Woe", Mainstream, 22: January1993, p. 15.

Purushottam, P., "A Profile of Beedi Workers", Social Change, 24: 1983, pp. 18-23.

Rakha Gupta and Bibin Kumar "Role of Women in Economic Development", Volume 31, No. 16, October 1-15, 1987.

Rajasekhar D., and Sreedhar G., "Alternative Employment for Women Beedi Workers: A Study in Dakshina Kanada District of Karnataka", Journal of Rural Development, 21(4), 2002, pp. 21-28.

Ramana Rao D.V.V., Impact of Institutional Credit on the Socio-economic Conditions of Rural Women in Self-help Groups", A Case Study in Bidar District of Karnataka, Rural Development, December, 2001.

Ramesh Chand, S.S., & Raju, L.M. Pandey and Surabhi Sonalkia, "Linkages between Urban Consumption and Rural Non-Farm Employment and Agriculture Income:

A New Perspective", Indian Journal of Agricultural Economics, Vol. 64, No. 3, 2009, pp. 409-420.

Rajasekhar, D. & Sreedhar. G., "Changing Face of Beedi Industry: A Study in Karnataka", Economic and Political Weekly, Vol. 37, No. 39, 2002, pp. 4023-4028.

Ravindran Nair. G.: "Women Workers Demand a Better Deal", Yojana, March 19-20, 1998.

Reena Jhabvalka and Shalink Sinha, "Social Security for Women Workers in the Unorganized Sector", The Indian Journal of Labour Economics,Vol. 44, No. 4, 2001, p. 577.

Rohni Nayar, "Female Participation Rates in Rural India", Economic and Political Weekly, Vol. 22, December 19, 1987, pp. 207-216.

Satya Sundaram. I., "Aspects of Rural Non-Farm Sector in India", Southern Economist, Vol. 46, No. 19, 2008, pp. 8-10.

Sandip Das., "Women Beedi Workers in Chattisgarh", Social Welfare., Vol. 50, No. 12, 2004, pp. 30-31.

Sebanti Ghosh., "Women Beedi Workers and Occupational Health Hazards", Women's Link, Vol. 16, No. 1, 2010, pp. 3-8.

Shyamala. A. & Haridoss. R., "Social Insurance Scheme for Unorganized Sector Workers", Southern Economist, Vol. 49, No. 5, 2010, pp. 15-19.

Sharma. H.R., "Rural Non-Farm Employment in Himachal Pradesh, 1971-2001-A District level Analysis", Indian Journal of Agriculture Economics, Vol. 64, No. 2, 2009, pp. 209-228.

Sreeja J.P., "Women and Occupational Hazards of Women Construction Workers in Selected Village of Agasteeswaram Taluk", Voice of the Hindecon, Vol. XII, Annual Publication, 2003, pp. 77-78.

Srinivasulu. K, "Impact of Liberalization on Beedi Workers", Economic and Political Weekly, Vol. 32, No. 11, 1997, pp. 515-517.

Shakuntala Balaraman,"Women Image making and Shaping over Throwing Stereo Types" Book Review, Economic and Political Weekly, 1986, Oct., p. 31.

Sumit Gupta and Mukta Gupta, "Women in India: Retrospect and Prospect", Women's World, 1989, No. 21-22, p. 4-5.

Sushila Srivastava and H. Sheriff, "Child Labour in Madras and Vellore", Social Welfare, 38: 1991, pp. 14-17.

Sukti Dasgupta. ,"Women Organizing for Socio-economic Security", Indian Journal of Labour Economics, Vol. 46, No. 1, 2003, pp. 39-53.

Vinish Kathiria, Rajesh Raj. S.N., Kunal Sen, "Organized versus Unorganized Manufacturing Performance in the Post – Reform Period", Economic and Political Weekly, Vol. 45, No. 24, 2010, pp. 55-64.

Vijayakumar. K. and Vanaja Rani. S: "Status of Women in Andhra Pradesh", Social Welfare Vol. 49, No. 8, November 2002, pp. 31-36.

Vijaya Kumar S. and Subhayamma G., "Social Security for Unorganized Sector in India, - A Need for Comprehensive Reforms" Indian Journal of Labour Economics, Vol. 4, No. 12, 2001, pp. 63-642.

Vivek Deo Lankar: "Status of Women Entrepreneurs", Khadi and Gramodyog (The Journal of Rural Economy) May 1985, p. 331.

Velayuthaperumal S.: "Profile of Rural Female Labour in India in Sudhir M.A and Balakrishnan, A (eds) Empowerment of Rural Women Labour Force", Annual Publications, New Delhi, 2002, p. 20.1.

Uma Rani Jeemol Unni, "Women Work and Insecurities in India ", Labour and Development, Vol. 10, No. 2, 2004, p. 107.

Unni Jeemol, "Employment and Wages among Rural Laboures, some Recent' Trends" Indian Journal of Agriculture Economics, Vol. 52, No. 1, January March, 1997, pp. 59-72.

REPORTS AND DOCUMENTS

District Statistical Hand Book 2009-2010, Thoothukudi District.

Labour Investigation Committee, Main Report, Government of India, 1994, p. 46.

Narayanasamy, B.V., "Report of the Court of Enquiry into Labour Conditions in Beedi, Cigar, Snuff, Tobacco-Curing and Tanning Industries", Government of India, 1969, pp. 40-45.

Planning Commission: "Social Welfare of India, Government of India", New Delhi, pp. 149-172.

Report of the Royal Commission on Labour, Government of India, 1929, p. 96.

Report on Occupational Health Issues of Women in the Unorganized Sector, New Delhi: The National Commission of Self-employed Women, 1988, p. 156.

Report of the Committee on Labour Welfare, Ministry of Labour, Government of India, 1969, pp. 59-70.

Report of the National Commission on Labour, Government of India, 1969, pp. 427-428.

Report of the Survey and Living of Beedi Workers, Ministry of Labour, Government of India, 1978, pp. 169-174.

Tamil Nadu – An Economic Appraisal, 2009-2010, Department of Evaluation and Applied Research (DEAR) Government of Tamil Nadu, Chennai, pp. S4 – S5.

THESIS ABSTRACTS

Amarjothi, "Human Resource Management of Match Industry in Sivakasi", Unpublished Ph.D. Thesis, Madurai Kamaraj University, Madurai, 2000.

Dissertation Abstracts International Vol. 69 No. 7 P. 2830A.

Gomathi V.: (1988), "A Study of Job Satisfaction of Women Employees in Public and Private Sector Banks in Tirunelveli Town", Unpublished Research Thesis, Madurai Kamaraj University, Madurai.

Gopalsamy R.; (1989) "A Study of Human Resource Management in Ramanathapuram District Central Co-operative Bank in Madurai", Unpublished Research Thesis, Madurai Kamaraj University, Madurai.

Kathiresan K.: Quoted by Rangachari N.R.: (1989) "A Study of Job Satisfaction of Employees of Paramakudi

Cooperative Weavers Society", Unpublished Research Thesis, Madurai Kamaraj University, Madurai.

Madasamy V., "A Study of the Problem of Production in Cottage Match Industrial Units in Kamaraj District", Unpublished Ph.D Thesis, Madurai Kamaraj University, Madurai, 1994.

Perumalammal (1981): "An Economic Study of Women Workers of Match Workers of Match Factories in Thayilpatti". Unpublished M.Phil Thesis, Madurai Kamarajar University, Madurai.

Ramalakshmi M : (1982) "An Economic Study of the Working and Living Conditions of the Women Labour in the Math Units in Virudhunagar", Unpublished M.Phil Thesis, Madurai Kamarajar University, Madurai.

Subhadra Patwa, "Comparative Study of Female and Male Workers in Diamond Trade and Industry", Unpublished Research Thesis, S.N.D.T. Women's University, Mumbai, Maharastra, 1994.

NEWS PAPERS

Indian Express; December 9, 1992, p. 9.

Kalpana Sharma, "Women in Perspective", Indian Express, 1988, July 31, p. 8.

Srirangatha, Opportunities in Rural Non-farm Sector, the Hindu December, 2004, p. 12.

FIELD VISIT REPORT

Field Visit Report on Child Labour, International Confederation of Free Trade Unions, Part I, South India, February 25 – March 4, 2002.

Field Visit Report on Child Labour, International Confederation of Free Trade Unions, Part II, Nepal, March 6 - 9, 2002.

WEB SITES

Chopra, the Economic Bondage of Brick Kiln Workers of Muzaffarnagar District in Uttar Pradesh, www.google.com, 1982.

Guerin Isabelle *et al.*, Labour in Brick Kilns: A Case Study in Chennai, www.google.com.

Gulati, A Case Study the Work and Family Life of Women in the Brick Industry, www.google.com, 1979.

Labour Bureau, Women Workers Employed in Brick Kilns in the North Indian States of Punjab and Haryana www.google.com, 1988.

Dharmalingam, Brick Workers in a Village in Tamil Nadu, www.google.com, 1995.

Singh, D.P., Women Workers in the Bricks Kiln Industry in Haryana, India, www.google.com

Index

* * * * * *